£7

41

224105

D1294246

To Greenland's Icy Mountains

BOOKS BY

EVE GARNETT

Is It Well With The Child?
(With a Foreword by Walter de la Mare and a
Preface by Marjorie Bowen)

AND FOR CHILDREN

The Family From One End Street
In and Out and Roundabout—Stories of a Little Town
A Book of the Seasons: An Anthology
Further Adventures of the Family From One End Street
Holiday at the Dew Drop Inn
(All illustrated by the author)

Hans Egede

To Greenland's Icy Mountains

The story of Hans Egede
Explorer, Coloniser, Missionary

EVE GARNETT

With a Foreword by Dr Nils Egede Bloch-Hoell
Lecturer in Theology in the University of Oslo

Illustrated with photographs and with drawings by the Author

'Every complete devotion to an idea yields some profit, even though it be different from that which was expected' . . . .

NANSEN

HEINEMANN : LONDON

William Heinemann Ltd

LONDON   MELBOURNE   TORONTO

CAPE TOWN   AUCKLAND

First published 1968
© Eve Garnett 1968
434 94052 6

Printed in Great Britain by
Clarke, Doble & Brendon Ltd
Cattedown, Plymouth

To all who have loved high latitudes, and gone down to the sea in ships to bring light into dark places.

CONTENTS

CONTENTS

ILLUSTRATIONS

FOREWORD

Do you remember the story about King Midas—The Golden Touch? Everything he touched turned into gold; food and drink and all that is necessary to uphold life were changed into gold, glittering, but *dead*. We don't envy King Midas. Even the roses lost their scent and life at the touch of his hand, and the King would have starved to death if the gift of the golden touch had not been taken away from him.

There is another gift, rare and precious, given to real artists, the gift of the *life-giving touch*. Eve Garnett has this gift. Whatever she draws and writes lives.

In this book Eve Garnett goes back in history to the eighteenth century. Or does she? I don't think so. Eve Garnett has picked the brave Norwegian *Hans Egede* out of history and made him and his family live. Yes, people and nature are living in this book, because the author has the life-giving touch.

When lecturing on church history I try to give the student an understanding of history. What did really happen, where and when, and why did it take place? Some students appreciate this. They are real students of history. I do not hesitate to say that Eve Garnett is a real student of history, and she has certainly spared no pains to find and present her facts. She combines in an admirable way faithfulness to historical accuracy with lively and imaginative art in telling the story. The saga of Hans Egede is simple enough to be enjoyed by children and will be read with pleasure by adults.

On behalf of the Egede descendants and in the name of church history I would like to express my gratitude for this book.

Holmenkollen, Norway
June 1967

Nils Egede Bloch-Hoell, D.D.

PREFACE

Outside Scandinavia and the Lutheran Church Hans Egede seems to be very little known. I do not know of any historically accurate book about him in English for children, and for adults only a translation of the official Danish 'Life' by the late Louis Bobé (Rosenkilde and Bagger 1952) and the contribution, 'History of the Mission' by H. Ostermann in 'Greenland', Vol. 3 (Oxford University Press 1929).

To Greenland's Icy Mountains is based solely on these two sources; on the extracts from Hans Egede's own writings quoted in them, and on information given me by his direct descendants. If to some readers the story is reminiscent of the pages of a Victorian Sunday School prize, I would like to say that this is intentional. Though written nearly 150 years earlier, all Hans Egede's books, diaries and correspondence have a strong mid-Victorian flavour. There is the same single-minded and fervent zeal; the stern—often harsh—discipline, the at times, and to modern ears, priggishly expressed piety, side by side with exuberance of spirit, unquestioning belief in progress, and unshaken faith in the future. Keeping as closely as possible to recorded facts, and using only such fiction as might be described as 'possible', I have tried to preserve this flavour. If *To Greenland's Icy Mountains* succeeds in making known to children of today the life and work of a remarkable and dauntless man—and his equally dauntless wife and family, it will have served its purpose.

To Danes and Norwegians who may read the book I offer my apologies for any omissions and inaccuracies (the last years excepted)—my only excuse the difficulty of working from translations, and my less than rudimentary knowledge of their languages.

Eve Garnett
Norway—England
July 1967

I

North of the Circle

PART ONE

Bishop Heber's hymn 'From Greenland's Icy Mountains' was more popular with our great-grandparents, or even our grandparents, than it is with ourselves. Also popular with them was a rather smug little saying, 'If at first you don't succeed, try, try again.'

There is a similar saying in Norwegian; young Hans Egede must have heard it often—too often he may have thought; yet the words, like the Icy Mountains, were to become part of his life.

Long before he was old enough to read the old Norse legends, Hans would listen entranced to their telling around the stove in his home in far off northern Norway. He thought of them by day; he dreamed of them by night. Floki, Erik-the-Red, Leif Ericsson; and the lands to which they sailed. Iceland, that strange, far away island; and Greenland—stranger still. Especially he dreamed of Greenland, remote, mysterious in the polar sea—the very end of all the earth!

Who was this boy, Hans Egede? (And before going further, for those who know no Danish or Norwegian I should explain that the name 'Egede' is pronounced '*Eh*-ghi-der', and not, as I fondly imagined when I first encountered it, '*Egg*-ede'!)

Hans Povelsen Egede—to give him his full name and the one by which he liked to call himself as a young man—was born on the last day of January in the year 1686 at Harstad on the island of Hinnöy, the largest of the many islands which fringe the northwest coast of Norway, and which lies some 100 miles across the arctic circle. His father, Povel Hansen, was a Dane, born also on an island—the island of Zeeland at the entrance to the Baltic Sea —'smiling Zeeland' as the Danes sometimes affectionately call it —where his father, (Hans' grandfather) Hans Jensen Coling, was vicar of the small township of Vester Egede.

Hans Jensen Coling was born in 1596—in the reign of our

1

Queen Elizabeth I. After serving the people of Vester Egede faithfully for thirty years, he died in 1659, leaving his wife, Kirsten Andersdatter with so large a family to care for that the vicar who succeeded to the living 'took pity' it is said, on the bewildered widow and married her.

Of the five sons of the family, Povel Hansen, eleven years old when his father died, was the youngest, and like the youngest son in so many fairy tales, the one to travel far afield when he grew up.

It is not known what made young Povel Hansen leave his stepfather's home or why, instead of the nearer and kindlier south, he chose the harsh and distant north, nor is there any record of his manner of reaching there. Almost certainly it must have been by boat. Roads, even today in North Norway, are few. In the seventeenth century they must have been almost non-existent. Then, as now, the greater part of transport—and indeed almost all communication, was by water, by little ships which pass easily in and out among the hundreds of islands and skerries that border the 1,600 mile Norwegian coastline between the Skagerak and the desolate North Cape.

All that is known for certain is that taking the name of Egede 'in memory of his native home', this son of the parsonage made his way to Norway, and 'some time later' entered the service of Jens Peter Hind, Sorenskriver* of Senjen in the far off Nordland province. Here, again in the fairy tale manner, he became betrothed to his master's daughter; was appointed his successor, and at his death a few years after their marriage, became Sorenskriver in his stead.

The official residence was at Harstad and here Povel Hansen and his wife Kirsten lived. Five children, three boys and two girls were born to them.

Hans was the second child, and the eldest son. He was baptized at the little fortress-like stone church at Trondenes a couple of miles from Harstad which, built early in the twelfth century, had long been proudly known as the 'Northernmost stronghold of Christianity'. The massive eight—in some parts twelve—feet thick stone walls stand little changed today, but who among those who stood within them on that dark and distant February day when the sun had only just begun to rise above the horizon

---

* Sorenskriver = at that time roughly corresponding to a Resident Magistrate of a country district.

for a brief hour or two after its long winter sleep, could have guessed that the—probably screaming (though we do not know!)—baby at the font, was to push that stronghold further, and ever further North.

'The names were Hans Povelsen', said one and another to their friends on their return home, 'Hans Povelsen Egede'.

'A dear little baby!' said others. 'He will grow up and one day succeed his father as Sorenskriver!'

The North-West winds swept roaring across the island.

'We heard!' they shrilled. 'We heard! But we know better! Hans Povelsen Egede—we know him. And he will learn to know us—well—very well! We shall visit him often! But he will leave Hinnöy. And one day he will visit us, and he will live among us—in our own home!'

And they swept onwards, rattling the timbers of the little wooden houses; bending the graceful birch trees to the ground, and making even the giant northern pines tremble.

And the newly-christened baby, now back in his wooden cradle at the homestead at Harstad, heard them as he lay sleeping; but he dreamed sweetly, as all newly-christened babies should surely do.

PART TWO

The baby grew up and after him came three more—first a sister and then two brothers.

Though their father held an important position he was poorly paid. Few of the islanders were rich and when the main source of income—the swirling shoals of herring—failed, as they sometimes did, he might have to wait many weeks for his salary.

But although his children knew poverty—even hunger—they also knew delight.

Life on the island of Hinnöy was hard. For a boy destined to live a harsh life in one of the worst climates in the world perhaps there could not have been a better training ground.

For nearly two months in winter the sun disappeared completely and only a greyish lightening of the sky for a few hours towards mid-morning told the difference between night and day. In a temperature where the thermometer frequently stood below zero* all activities had to be carried out by the flickering light of lanterns or the glare of rush lights or torches, and in the waist-

* Fahrenheit used throughout.

3

deep snow which sometimes drifted halfway up the small wooden houses.

On the bleak south and south-west coasts mountainous waves hurled themselves against the razor-like rocks of the skerries and broke with a roar on desolate grey stone beaches, drowning the cries of seabirds, flinging weed and driftwood high in the air, and sending showers of salt spray flying far inland. By comparison, conditions on the eastern coast, where the little township of Harstad lay tucked away at the northern end, were almost kindly.

Snow and frost, and the long darkness were there too, and, as already said, the north-west winds blew roaring over the houses, but encircling mountains and small birch and fir woods sheltered the town from the worst of the weather. And there were many compensations: skiing and sledging on the lower slopes of the mountains and on what in summer was surprisingly rich pasture land; skating on the small lakes under stars grown mysteriously bright; and often—sometimes night after night—a wild glory in the sky! Great curtains of green and red light folding and unfolding; long streamers of saffron and violet, orange and blue; lights shooting across the sky, rising here, falling there like some gigantic firework display. The magic of the Aurora Borealis—the 'Northern Lights'!

But even the enchantment of the Aurora was challenged by the coming of spring. On the day when the whole of the sun's disc showed above the horizon for the first time, even the very poorest had a celebration of some kind.

Every day now something was happening; daylight lengthening; snow turning soft and moist; the drip, drip, drip, of icicles; and from the frozen waterfalls the faint trickling sound of water beginning to flow again. Hibernating animals woke from their winter sleep and droves of small twittering birds appeared overnight. Everywhere life was stirring.

It was not all happiness of course. There were discomforts; instead of snow there was often cold, driving rain; everything dripped and leaked. No skiing or skating was possible and every road and track was deep in muddy slush. But wet, or dry, the days were growing longer, the sun on one's face warmer; tops of small trees emerged through the melting snow. Very soon pale grey-green buds on the willow and birch scrub were showing

4

here and there; tiny blades pushing up through boggy turf, and one day some child would cry 'A flower! A flower!' and everyone who could would rush to see it. Spring had come!

In a week or two, though the snow lingered here and there and was still deep on the mountains, the first flower had become one of millions; little mosaics of brilliant colour among the spearing blades of emerald grass in the pastures; pushing up through last year's leaves in the birch woods; bordering the roadsides. Small alpine flowers, but among them anemones, heartsease-pansies, dog-violets and many others well known in warmer lands.

And slowly day by day, summer—the season that everyone talked of . . . longed for . . . drew nearer.

The smaller children could not even remember what summer was like, but they waited for it eagerly, impatiently, asking every day 'How long now?' as an English child might wait for and ask about Christmas.

And when summer *did* come—unless as sometimes happened it was a particularly disappointing one, rainy, cloudy, or uncertain, with a day or two of high promise ending in gales or thunderstorms—it was all that everyone had longed for.

From the end of May to late July, darkness vanished. At eleven o'clock at night, sinking low in the sky but never touching the horizon, the sun shone brilliantly. Before midnight sunset and sunrise had become one and it was climbing upwards again. At one, two, three o'clock in the morning people were still strolling about or working in the fields. Children, all normal bedtime abandoned, played un-rebuked in the brilliant rays.

There was an incessant activity, a constant coming and going. It was as if no one could bear to waste a moment, must live to the full every hour before the long darkness should come again. Cut off from all communication for so many months, friends and relations went visiting each other all over the island; to other islands, across to the mainland.

Besides the usual fishing on the sea there was fishing in the lakes and rivers. Great catches of salmon, their silver scales gleaming in the midnight sunbeams, lay on the grey stones. There were excursions to the woods in search of wild strawberries; up the mountains for berries.

5

In the clear, sharp air the sound of bells cling-clanged as cows and goats with newly born calves and kids were released from dark stuffy byres to pasture in meadows and on the lower mountain slopes. The arctic hares shed their white winter coats and turned browner every day; new birds arrived, more animals re-appeared.

On the lakes, in and out of the skerries, hundreds of little eider ducks swam in trim formation one behind the other like a tiny fleet, diving when their leader dived, remaining submerged and surfacing—though never where you expected—all together.

Grass and crops grew with amazing rapidity; the shining banners of the bog cotton waved on the marshes, and bordering every road and track, white now with powdery dust, tall flowers— big yellow trollius like curled pats of creamy butter, and deep purple monkshood, replaced the little, earlier flowers.

Everywhere life teemed. Summer had come!

It must have been in this joyful season that the young Hans Egede began his first lessons. Though his father was not a scholar himself, much of the clergyman's son remained in him and in spite of his poor circumstances he was determined to do everything possible to educate his children to the standard that had prevailed in his own vicarage home.

Hans' first teachers were his uncle Peter Hind—his mother's brother, then curate of the little fortress-like church at Trondenes, and later Niels Schjelderup, the vicar of Hamaröy, a small township on the mainland further down the coast.

Hans probably enjoyed these lessons, and would certainly have thought nothing of the two and a half mile walk from Harstad— possibly twice a day—even in winter.

His uncle's parsonage was pleasant; well-furnished compared with his own poor home. Tables and benches of polished birchwood; big chests covered with carving, and a carved chair for his uncle. Shining pewter plates and mugs to eat and drink from, and in the kitchen gleaming copper ladles and pans. And—best of all—books; big, leather-bound books.

Except in the homes of the clergy and of rich men, books were rare in those days—particularly rare in remote islands like Hinnöy. In Hans' own home there was probably only the Bible, a Latin primer and some old Norse legends.

In summer at the vicarage it was cool in the long, low-ceilinged living-room; in winter a warm and welcome refuge from the darkness and snow.

Lessons went happily in such surroundings and we know Hans must have learnt well and thoroughly, both with his uncle and with Niels Schjelderup at Hamaröy for the next thing history tells of him he is ready to pass the entrance examination to the University at far-off Copenhagen. He is eighteen years old. The year is 1704; Queen Anne sits on the throne of England; a new century has begun.

The little church at Trondenes is hardly changed. A farm stands on the site of the old vicarage, but mountains and skies, skerries and lakes—even the rough unsurfaced road along which the boy Egede tramped to lessons with his uncle are still as he must have known them. Children play today on the rough road and around the old church as thrilled with the re-appearance of the sun, the first spring flower, and the long light summer nights as Hans and his sisters and brothers over two hundred years ago.

2

South of the Circle

PART ONE

The University of Copenhagen; why Copenhagen you may ask?
Hans Egede lived in Norway; were there no Universities there?
The answer is there were not.

At that time Norway and Denmark were one kingdom under
the rule of a Danish King—at that particular date King
Frederik the Fourth. The chief seat of learning and the nearest
place where a degree could be obtained was Copenhagen. The
founding of the University of Oslo—or Christiania as it was then
called—lay more than a hundred years ahead; a dream, a small
hope stirring in the minds of a few scholars.

To the young Hans Egede who had hardly been out of his
own northern island it must have been a great and exciting
adventure to start off on the long journey south. But there was
sadness mingled with the excitement; the thought of leaving his
home; his parents, his sisters and his two young brothers. His
father was an old man now; he had not grown much richer
with the years and his health was failing. To save enough to send
this eldest son away to Copenhagen had meant a hard struggle
and Hans was well aware of this. The bustle and preparation for
his journey had helped to keep his spirits up, but at the last,
standing on the deck of the little schooner that was to carry
him southwards, and looking down on the small group of family
and friends clustered together on the jetty below, he was suddenly
engulfed in a wave of desolation . . . fear of the unknown and
far away . . . of separation . . . of failure . . .

'Write'! he had called despairingly as the sailors began drawing up the gangway and severing the last small link with land.
'Write! Write *often*!' and then was ashamed . . . Letters cost so
much to send. But the wind blowing strongly from the shore blew
his words back to him. Grateful, he stood waving, waving, as the
space between ship and jetty slowly widened.

Letters would come, he knew. His mother had prom-

8

ised to try and send one every month. She would tell him most of what he longed to know; of his father's health; how the crops and young animals fared; and the progress—or otherwise—of his young brothers' education, in which he had recently been taking a hand and which was a matter very near to his heart.

'Try and make *some* headway—especially with your Latin and arithmetic', he had sternly admonished the elder—and lazier—of the two, twelve-and-a-half-year-old Jens. 'And you'—to seven-year-old Christian, '*you* I shall expect to be able to read fluently by the time I return!'

Karen, his younger sister, had promised 'a line' enclosed in her mother's letters, and 'a line' and no more Hans knew well enough was exactly what it would be. Karen, as she always gaily admitted, preferred a rolling-pin or carding-comb to what she called 'labouring with a pen'.

Kirsten, his elder sister, had not long married. Though her home was some distance from Harstad, it was near enough for her to visit her family now and then, and, unlike Karen, writing was no labour to her. Pen and paper, rolling-pin or carding-comb, she was equally at home with them all. His newly acquired brother-in-law Hans did not know very well, but well enough to be sure he would do his best to help the family, especially the younger ones, should their own father be unable to do so . . .

The figures on the jetty were very small now . . . Hans stood looking until they were tiny specks . . . until the little schooner headed seawards, the mountains closed in and they were hidden from view. Then he turned himself about, set his jaw—that formidable Egede jaw—and vowed a vow. There might be fear—but there would be no failure! He would work—and work—and *work*! He would show his fellow students what sort of beings came from north of the Circle! And picking up the small corded wooden chest containing his few belongings in one hand, and a little bundle of food in the other, he went below.

The vow taken on the schooner was kept. After passing his entrance examination to the University Hans gave himself a week to search out various friends of his father living in and around Copenhagen, and to see some of the sights of the town. Then he set to work on his chosen course.

9

It was only during the last few months he had made up his mind what profession he would follow. The choice had not been easy; he had so many interests!

'Too many irons in the fire', his father sometimes complained—little knowing how valuable many, if not all, these 'irons' would one day be to his son.

Chemistry and geology were two of them. Hans was always hoping to discover some precious herb or valuable metal. His mother frequently complained that his bedroom looked as if the sea had washed over it during the night, it was so full of sand and stones and sinister-looking lumps of rock!

Surveying was another 'iron'. The 'lie' of any particular piece of land, heights and contours of mountains fascinated him. Whenever he went to any new place, however small and remote and unimportant, he drew a map of it. He drew well and often made little pictures of trolls—the Norwegian fairies and gnomes—and of birds and animals for his young brothers.

Fishing and farming had been bound up with his life ever since he could remember and he liked experimenting in these matters—particularly with crops. The experiments frequently resulted in failure—and, more disastrous, a waste of the scanty supply of land available for cultivation. Then his father would do more than complain; he would become angry and there would be no more experiments—till next time.

History, mathematics and astronomy—all attracted Hans, and he had a very real facility for languages. Many choices were open to him. There was one thing, however, in which he was never interested. This was in the making of money; that is, the making of money for its own sake. He knew its value—none better,—his childhood had been bitterly hard for want of it—and that it was not to be despised. But it was a subject on which he felt strongly and though throughout the whole of his life he was to be hampered by lack of it, he never changed his views. People and things—particularly people, came first with him always.

Although he had always secretly cherished the hope that one at least of his children might enter the church, Hans' father very wisely made no attempt to influence his son's choice of career, indeed, when Hans at last told him his mind was made up and he wished to be a priest like his grandfather, he was troubled. Hans was a fine lad, but he could be stubborn as a mule. He was also subject to sudden, and sometimes violent, fits of temper. It is true the strict Lutheran clergy of those days were given to outbursts of wrath against erring parishioners—sometimes even resorting to what were described as 'chastisements'! Even so, his father had misgivings whether Hans with his restless energy and enquiring mind was suited to the monotonous and often lonely life of a remote country parish. If he could have peeped into the future and seen this stubborn son of his refuse the Bishopric of Trondheim, and, two centuries later become the subject of altar-piece and statue here in his native Harstad, it is doubtful whether he would have believed—or indeed even approved it!

Whether Hans himself was fully aware of the questing, restless spirit within him, there is no record. Nor that he had any particular ambitions or any thought of a livelihood other than the stay-put hard-working life of a parish priest. As to being a missionary . . .

It is true there was a revival of interest in overseas missions during the time he was in Copenhagen, and it is believed that he was present at the ordination of two priests and among the crowd that gathered to cheer their departure to the East Indies. A letter written some years later and still preserved, shows that he followed their careers with interest; but there is no evidence whatever that the idea of being a missionary himself ever entered his head. To be told he would one day be known as 'The Apostle of Greenland' would certainly have been very surprising to him!

The days at the University flew by. The longed for letters from home came fairly frequently and all seemed well there. But they gave no news of improvement in his father's health, and Hans was more than ever determined to take his degree in the shortest possible time. It is known that he worked very hard, and he can have had little liesure—and certainly little money for amusements.

With his many interests he soon found other students with whom he could talk and argue and discuss things—often far into the night, or, when he could snatch the time, on long country walks.

At the end of only eighteen months, he sat for his Bachelor's Degree in Theology, and daily, for close on a week, from early morning to late afternoon, in company with several dozen other

11

young men, sat scribbling hard in the examination hall of the University.

Then came the agonising period of suspense known to all students waiting to learn their fate—to know whether they have passed or failed.

There is no record of it, but it is very likely that during this anxious time Hans visited his grandparents' old home at Vester Egede about fifty miles from Copenhagen, and if so that he drew one of his little maps so that his father might see some of the changes—how trees had grown, farms and houses been built—in the many years that had passed since, as a young man, he had left to seek his fortune in Norway.

At last the long waiting time came to an end. The day arrived when the examination results were posted up in the main Hall of the University and the students came thronging in to learn their fate.

Almost before he had had time to read the list, Hans was being clapped on the back, congratulated, shaken by the hand!

He had passed! Not with distinction of any kind, not even very well, but passed!

Anything better was hardly to be expected in the brief time he had set himself. This was confirmed by his professors in a testimonial they wrote for him, adding the tribute that 'anyone who knew his hard-working thoroughness could not wonder that he had passed his examination at such an early age'.

He was not quite twenty years old.

Hans was only too thankful to have passed at all! Now he could be ordained, and earn his living, and should his father's health fail completely, help to support the family. He was all impatience to be home. He counted out what money he had left, and putting aside enough to keep him until his ship should sail, and for the voyage itself, set himself to wait with such patience as he could muster.

It was only now, when he had time and leisure to contemplate the neat, flat fields and gently swelling little hills round Copenhagen that he realised fully how deeply he had missed his native mountains. Though the climate might be less hard, the winters shorter, the trees and flowers finer here in Denmark, he ached for Hinnöy with its bleak stone beaches, its windswept lakes, its pines and birch trees, and small, delicate flowers.

His last day in Copenhagen, he spent prowling among the

market booths buying little presents for his family. An embroidered handkerchief for his mother; necklaces for his sisters; a fine quill pen for his father; and, smiling rather wryly, uncertain how such a gift might be received, a writing book each for Jens and young Christian.

Early the next morning to the cheers and waving of many student friends he boarded his ship and sailed for the north.

To the anxious-to-be-home young man the long voyage seemed even longer than it was. There were so many little ports to be called at, so many goods to be taken on or put off; boxes and bales of merchandise; barrels of fish; livestock—cocks and hens, some sheep, a goat; even a little light-cocoa-coloured horse, its long mane and tail blowing like banners in the breeze as it was swung aloft and lowered gently into a waiting wooden box.

All too frequently Hans was reminded of St. Paul—another impatient traveller who had found the winds 'contrary unto him'; and there were many days when there was no wind at all.

Slowly the little ship made her way up the lovely mountain-guarded coast where the deep snows of winter were still unmelted, carefully threading her way among the myriads of skerries and small islands. The mountains became steeper, their rocky, jagged summits rising sheer above the deep snow-fields on the upper slopes.

Early one morning the sharp air blew colder—ice in its breath. They were nearing the coast that hides the great Svartisen glacier. In a few hours now the Circle would be crossed; another two days—three days—then Hinnöy—and home!

There were heavy showers during the early morning of the last day on board but as they neared Harstad the sun came out and a magnificent rainbow spanned the harbour. Like two great men still to be born, Wordsworth the poet and Constable the painter, Hans Egede loved a rainbow. It was the perfect welcome home.

A fishing boat had brought the news that the schooner was arriving, and on the little jetty stood his whole family. His mother, her white kerchief gleaming in the sunshine, smiling for joy that this longed for day had really come; his father leaning on a stick, one arm through that of his elder daughter. He too was smiling, but the briefest glance showed how bent and old he had grown. On his other side stood Karen waving excitedly, and hovering

13

near her Jens—now a lanky fourteen-year-old—grinning from ear to ear! As for young Christian, Hans hardly knew him! From being a round, podgy, little boy he had grown tall and slim—graceful as the young saplings that grew beside the landing stage.

Within a few months of Hans' home-coming his father died.

Sad as he was he had little time to think about his grief. His father's salary had always been insufficient and latterly he had grown too old and feeble to continue with the only means he had of adding to it—fishing in one of his square-rigged coasters, and cultivating his little farm.

Now even the small salary had stopped and bills and payments of every kind were accumulating.

All his goods were mustered and put up for sale.

A document containing a list of these and their value still exists. 'Of silver 2 tankards, 3 brandy bowls, 3 goblets and 15 spoons . . . Pewter, brass, ore and copper utensils; merchandise; fish-sawing implements and other movables; bedclothing, cloths for tables and cushions for benches . . . linen; livestock; two square-rigged coasters . . .'

In all, the value amounted to 1,106 Rigsdaler (about £220) while the debts were estimated at 1,401 Rigsdaler.

In legal language 'the liabilities exceeded the assets' or, as a Danish historian bluntly puts it 'there was less than nothing for the heirs'.

A sad and worrying time must have followed. With 'less than nothing' debts had to be paid and the Egede family fed, clothed and housed. Where, how, and on what they existed we do not know, but the greater part of the burden of dealing with everything must certainly have fallen on Hans.

Very likely Kirsten and her husband provided a roof and helped with the education of Jens and Christian. Hans himself had a benefactor in Peder Krogh the Bishop of Trondheim, who owned what in England would be called the 'gift' of various livings in his diocese among which were the Lofoten Islands, and parts of Hinnöy.

On the 15th April 1707, almost exactly a year after his father's death, Hans Egede was ordained. A few weeks later he was appointed to the living of Vaagan—a district of the Lofoten Islands which lie to the south-west of Hinnöy out in the North Atlantic;

14

the last land in North West Europe and famous from Viking days
for its fisheries.

PART TWO

'In the year he was ordained, Hans Egede married Gertrud
Rasch, daughter of Niels Rasch, of Kvæfiord'.

This brief statement is almost all we know concerning what
was to prove one of the most important events in Hans Egede's
life. The happiest of marriages, it was to influence not only his
own future, but that of a vast and distant country, the lives of
hundreds of men and women, and of children yet unborn.

One has only to look at the portrait of Gertrud Rask—as
she always signed herself—to see she was a woman of outstand-
ing character; kindly, capable of unswerving devotion, and, most
certainly the possessor of a strong sense of humour—all qualities
that would be needed, and tested to the utmost, in ways of which
she could never possibly have dreamed.

Gertrud Rasch was thirteen years older than her husband and
as poor as he! It was very definitely a love match. And in love,
and faith, early in the following year they set sail together for
Lofoten.

They landed at Svolvær, the largest of the Island's harbours
and chief port of the fisheries. The Vaagan vicarage was some
six miles away, just outside Kabelvåg, a small but endlessly busy
little fishing village. To reach it meant a further journey in another, smaller ship.

There were no roads, only a rough, lonely twisting track, that
wound up and down hill, without a sign of any habitation, in
places not unlike Hinnöy, and with occasional glimpses of sea
between the mountains. Today a road has replaced the track;
cars, lorries, and the bus taking children to school in Svolvær drive
along it, but otherwise it is almost as winding and lonely as it was
over two hundred years ago.

Hans and his bride found the vicarage and the little wooden
church near it very dilapidated and sadly in need of repair, but
the surroundings were of an enchanting beauty—a beauty,
especially looking seawards, in which there seemed some strange,
dream-like quality.

Immediately behind the vicarage rose a high range of rocky

15

mountains, below them rough boulder-strewn slopes covered with scrub and small birch trees.

Little streams trickled in and out among the boulders, or poured over them in miniature waterfalls, but wherever a flat surface presented itself the scrub had been cleared and the precious soil cultivated.

Close to the house itself was a tiny orchard, gay in season with apple and cherry trees, and a patch of garden with currant bushes and vegetables.

Across the road which passed the garden gate, was a stretch of swampy grassland where some of the little streams converged in one large one. Yellow in spring and early summer with myriads of marsh-marigolds, it ended in low rocky cliffs and a huddle of big grey boulders spilling over onto a series of small sandy beaches.

Except at low tide these little beaches were divided from each other by ridges of high rocks; the lower ridges were covered with thick, slippery, yellow-brown seaweed, and the ebb tides left small shallow pools around them.

Far out on the horizon lay the high mountain ranges of neighbouring islands, and away to the west the giant peak

Vågekallen—subject of many a tale and legend—its summit and upper slopes still white with snow.

Where the marsh ended, a rough track branched off from the road leading towards the cliffs and a few fishermen's huts which stood half-hidden by row upon row of high wooden fish racks on which the cod hung to dry, as it does, all over the Islands, to this day.

16

The road itself climbed steeply, then turned abruptly and ran downhill to Kabelvåg, a scatter of little wooden houses, jetties, small warehouses, and everywhere, drying fish. Beyond it towered Vågekallen in all his glory.

A paltry salary, the poorest of parishioners, a dilapidated dwelling . . .

Hans and his bride cared nothing! They had work to do; a home; a home set in unsurpassed beauty. . . . When Hans read the evening prayers that first night in the Islands, they both gave special thanks for each of these three things.

3

The Idea Comes

One October evening, some months after his arrival in Lofoten, the vicar of Vaagan was walking on his favourite beach.

The weather was calm and still. He stopped for a moment and stood looking towards the high chains of fantastically shaped mountains lying mistily blue on the horizon, their summits already streaked with the first snow of winter, and his thoughts went out to the vast stretches of ocean beyond them and the lands which lay there . . . Iceland . . . Greenland . . .

And immediately Hans Egede was a boy again, listening to the old Norse legends around the stove in the homestead at Harstad on long winter nights.

Never forgotten, absorbed into the very fibre of his being, to him they had never been legend but fact, and now, as he wrote in one of his diaries, suddenly he was filled with a burning curiosity, a strange, intense longing, to know what had become of the descendants of those old Norsemen—those first adventurers to Greenland and the polar seas.

He knew, as every educated Norwegian of his time, the history of his country's once thriving, now half-forgotten, almost lost, colony. How the immense frozen land was first sighted; all the details of its flourishing early history enshrined in the beloved sagas; the gradually dwindling communications in later centuries; the ever faltering stream of information; the thin trickle of news today—tales told by the crews of occasional foreign traders; short entries in log book or diary of Danish and Norwegian whaling skippers.

Still gazing seawards, all he had ever read of Greenland passed slowly through his mind like some long forgotten dream, now sharp and distinct, now vague and shadowy.

The sparse history of this strange, vast country—now known to be the largest island in the world, begins about the year 900 when an Icelander named Gunnbjorn, blown off course in a

18

storm, sighted clearly and in all their majesty the towering ice cliffs of the eastern coast.

Some seventy years later, a Norwegian—known always as Erik-the-Red on account of his flaming hair and beard—who had quarrelled, killed, and been outlawed from Norway, settled in Iceland. He cleared land, married and lived peaceably for a time; then he quarrelled and killed again.

Once more an outlaw, unable to return to Norway, unable to remain in Iceland, only one course was open to him—to sail westward and try to discover the land Gunnbjorn had seen.

In the summer of 983, with his family, retainers, and a few friends he set sail for the unknown.

Like every traveller in the region he soon encountered the great belt of drift-ice which lies for hundreds of miles along the east Greenland coast, 'narrow enough for ships outside it to see the land but so thick and dense it is almost impossible to force a way through it'.*

Having no doubt made several attempts to do this and failed, Eric sailed southwards for about four hundred miles, rounded what is now Cape Farewell, and after exploring hundreds of barren islands and desolate fiords at last found land that appeared habitable; good pasturage; small stunted trees; an abundance of berries.

Well satisfied, he spent two years exploring further. He found no human beings but traces of dwellings known today to have been the homes of the first inhabitants—roving bands of eskimos from North America in pursuit of migrating animals.

By the third summer, having decided the land was worthy of settlement, Erik returned to Iceland under, it is supposed, the protection of some powerful friend.

He called the new-found country Greenland 'because', as he said, 'with such a name people will be more easily persuaded to go there!'

Whether due to this strategem or not there seem to have been plenty of volunteers, for later in the same summer he sailed back, accompanied by twenty-five ships laden with eager emigrants, their families and household goods; horses, cattle, sheep and goats and stores of all kinds.

But alas, of the twenty-five ships that sailed, only fourteen arrived. Some of the travellers—intimidated perhaps by the for-

* Rink: Danish Greenland.

19

bidding look of the icy mountains and the apparently unbroken whiteness of the so-called Greenland, turned back. Others were lost; in the ice; in mountainous seas.

Erik himself was a superb navigator, sailing in the open, un-decked ships of the time, without compass, reckoning only by sun, moon and stars, some of the most dangerous seas in the world. He was also a great leader. He soon had the surviving emigrants building houses; tilling the soil in the rocky valleys; hunting seal and bear.

Very soon more settlers came from Iceland and the colony grew and flourished. It was known as East Bygd.

Erik explored further but found nowhere suitable for settlement except along the narrow coastal strip and the shores of the more sheltered fiords. Whatever the interior of the land, it was inaccessible; the icy mountains stood guard, range upon range of them, aloof, implacable.

The years went by. Erik's young son Leif grew to manhood and in the year 999 set sail for Norway to invite some of their own countrymen to join them.

A great, if not greater navigator than his father, Leif Erikson was, in the words of his famous countryman, Fridtjof Nansen, 'the first ocean voyager who deliberately and with a settled plan steered straight across the Atlantic; . . . with the compass unknown and in open-decked ships, an exploit equal to the greatest in history . . .'*

While in Norway, Leif came under the influence of King Olaf, then converting his country to Christianity. He was baptised, and when he returned to Greenland in the year 1,000 among those who sailed with him were 'a priest and other teachers'† sent by the King to preach the gospel in the newly settled land.

By now Erik was growing old and the undisputed head of a large, free and thriving state. He did not take kindly to the missionaries from Norway and refused, it is said, to become a Christian though his wife Thodhilda was baptised and 'at once built a small church' though not, adds the Saga, 'overnear their house' !†

In the winter of the same year Erik died.

As the years passed more and more colonists arrived from Norway. East Bygd spread into many new settlements and others

* In Northern Mists.
† Olaf's Saga IV.

sprang up further north eventually becoming known as West Bygd. Farms and homesteads increased, churches were built.

Life for the settlers, if not luxurious, was reasonably comfortable. There were horses and cattle, sheep and goats; hay in the barns; catches of seal and walrus—sometimes even a whale.

But the colonies were never entirely self-supporting. Any luxuries and necessities such as corn—which even today cannot be induced to ripen in the brief Greenland summer—and timber for house and boat building, had to be brought by ships from Norway.

By the year 1125 a Norwegian bishop had been appointed, founded his see at Garda and built what was to become the cathedral church of St. Nicholas.

As time went on the farms and homesteads grew into little townships; by the middle of the next century there is known to have been a population of about 3,000, some hundred and eighty farms, and sixteen churches.

So thriving and prosperous were the settlers that they decided to assert their independence and rebel against paying taxes to the King of Norway.

But the rebellion was short-lived. A fleet of ships sent by the angry King, Magnus VI, soon appeared on the horizon, and at this alarming sight, fearful no doubt that future supplies might be cut off, the rebels gave in.

A treaty was signed and for nearly another hundred years peace reigned. Both East and West Bygd continued to thrive and then suddenly they began to decline. By the end of the century—less than forty years—the spreading townships, farms, homesteads and their inhabitants, the bishop, the priests and the sixteen churches were gone! Vanished like dew before the summer sun! Gone, before long, almost the memory of them while the sagas which were their history came to be thought of as idle tales—at best legend.

The old sailing routes were deserted; desolate seas that had begun to grow familiar were desolate once again . . . Greenland's icy mountains were seen no more.

What exactly happened? Even today no one can say for certain. It is known that during the fourteenth century the wealth and power of the Danish kings began to fail. Fewer ships sailed to Greenland and after the outbreak of the Black Death in Europe in 1348 fewer still.

By 1397 when Norway and Denmark became one under Danish rule, a ship from Europe was already a rare sight; before the end of the next century the Pope noted that no ship had visited Greenland for eighty years.

The Black Death probably reached Greenland too, killing many and so weakening the survivors that little by little, cut off from vital supplies, their strength was sapped and gradually failed—graves recently examined show relics of Christian burial but the skeletons in them are not those of tall and hearty old Vikings but of very small men and women, young, rickety and under-nourished.

There is some evidence too that about this time the climate became very much colder. Crops failed to ripen and bears and other animals from the far north migrated southwards pursued—as in the days before Erik-the-Red—by roving eskimos from North America—hunters—independent of crops.

Clashes with the remaining and weakened settlers may well have occurred. Grim legends handed down from generation to generation hint at dark deeds and terrible scenes of slaughter.

Whatever the cause, or causes, the settlements and their inhabitants vanished, utterly and completely, and many long arctic winters and short arctic summers—one hundred and fifty of them—were to go by before Greenland's icy mountains were seen again by any European.

During those years had the last descendants of the Christian settlers died—the only white men in a vast, almost forgotten white land?

This Hans Egede firmly refused to believe—and for a reason that will be told later.

It was left to an Englishman to bring the next news of Greenland.

In the early summer of 1576 Martin Frobisher, a sailor in the service of Queen Elizabeth the First, convinced of the existence of the fabled North West Passage—the long-desired short cut to India and the East—set sail in search of it. He sighted the mountains of Greenland's southern-most tip—'like pinnacles of steeples all covered with snow',* he wrote, but was unable to land because of the ice.

In the two following years he returned but each time sailed

* Sir John Barrow: 'Voyages into the Arctic Regions'.

22

home without success, beaten by violent storms, fog, drifting ice.

At the time his voyages were considered complete and dismal failures but interest in the North West Passage had been stimulated and eight years later, John Davis, one of the greatest sailors of all time, was sent by the Queen with two ships and instructions to search for it. Rounding the south-eastern coast of Greenland, Davis sailed northwards up the strait which today bears his name and landed near the present capital, Godthaab.

He found some friendly eskimos, whom he treated with respect and quickly won their affection by ordering his sailors to dance for them! He contented himself with a brief exploration, noting carefully, as was his way, details of the country and the manner of life of the inhabitants, and at the end of the short summer sailed for home.

The next year he returned with four ships, two of which he despatched up the east Greenland coast. These were quickly in difficulties in the ice and unable to advance sailed for home.

Davis himself had tried to land on the southernmost tip but, like Frobisher before him, was unable to penetrate the ice and naming the spot Cape Farewell he sailed northwards landing again near Godthaab. Exceptionally thick ice that year prevented further exploration north but in spite of persistent fogs, mist and cold he managed to cruise in and out of fiords again noting carefully all he saw.

But time was short, the weather showed no sign of relenting, and sending one ship home Davis sailed in the other to the American shore tracing the coast southwards for hundreds of miles and noting amongst other things the richness of the fishing grounds off Newfoundland.

But still the North West Passage was not found and the following year Davis sailed north again. This year the weather was better, the sea near Godthaab almost ice free, and he managed to sail a little beyond 72° north. Here he saw 'open sea both to the north and west' but almost immediately was driven back by ferocious northerly gales.

He arrived home to find England tensely awaiting the Spanish Armada. Further exploration was impossible; the search for the North West Passage abandoned.

Davis published two books about his voyages, and his influence on all further arctic exploration was enormous. In the words of a modern explorer he had 'lighted Hudson into his strait. . . . Baffin into his bay'.* He had also, as we should say today, 'put Greenland on the map'.

It was not long before news of Davis's prowess reached the King of Denmark. Indifferent to the North West Passage, King Christian IV was curious and faintly troubled about the fate of the old Norse colonists. He also believed valuable minerals—possibly gold—might be hidden in the long neglected land. In the year 1603 he despatched ships under English commanders with instructions to search for both colonies and gold.

No colonies were found, but some lumps of shining metal looked promising.

A second expedition sailed in the following year. Still no trace of colonies—or colonists—was found, and the metal with which the ships were greedily, even dangerously, loaded proved only too well the truth of the old proverb that all that glitters is by no means gold.

A third expedition in 1603 brought only disaster, loss of a ship and many men, and eventually, the King's interest.

Other interests, however, had been aroused. Shrewd merchants began to suspect gold of another kind might be found in the teeming northern seas. Expeditions were eagerly equipped and for the next hundred years, Danes and Dutchmen particularly, strove with each other for supremacy in whaling and sealing.

* Sir Clements Markham: 'The Lands of Silence'.

Sailors from Bergen and Copenhagen were nearly always forthcoming for these enterprises. Small trading posts with the eskimos on Greenland's western coasts were established, but with few exceptions—plans that came to nothing, expeditions that never sailed—not another thought seems to have been given by their countrymen to their long lost colonies, or colonists!

And so things remained when a young vicar stood staring seawards on a little lonely beach in far away Lofoten.

4

Try, try, again!

'From that hour', wrote Hans Egede in his diary, 'an inner Voice never left me'. And he adds that as he stood gazing, musing about polar seas, and, he admits, at first more curious than concerned about the fate of his long-lost countrymen, he was suddenly aware—aware in his innermost being—as aware as if it had been shouted from the roofs of the fishermen's huts beside the cod-racks on the cliff above—that he, Hans Egede, was the man chosen, appointed, destined—call it what you will—to search for the descendants of those old and Christian countrymen. Christians still? Men struggling to keep their faith among hordes of heathen savages, or, abandoned over the centuries, cut off from their church, heathens now themselves; sunk in savagery; worshipping strange and barbarous gods?

The very thoought had suddenly become unendurable to him.

In the golden evening light he walked home, not briskly as was his way, but as a man in a dream; and he went quietly into the house instead of bursting in in his usual impetuous manner, calling his latest observations or little scraps of news. Throughout the evening meal he was silent and absorbed and though after it he settled down to read as usual, his wife, sitting opposite him with her sewing, observed that he never opened his book. She asked no questions but every now and then she glanced up at him and each time she was struck afresh by the shining light in his eyes; a strange radiance that seemed to envelop him.

'He looks', she said to herself, 'as if he had seen a vision!' Being a practical woman, however, as well as a discerning one, she went on with her sewing, but like Mary of old she 'pondered these things in her heart'.

Many times in the long years ahead and in the savage bleakness of an unknown and barren country, she was to be reminded

26

of that golden October evening; of the wrapt and radiant look on the face of her young husband, and to draw strength and courage from it.

'An inner Voice never left me'. This does not mean that the vicar of Vaagan sat down and thought about nothing else. He was a practical man and he had work to do—and plenty of it; but in his more leisured moments—walking to nearby villages, sailing between the islands which made up his widely scattered parish, the Voice nagged. At night, unable to sleep, or lying awake in the early morning hours when all worries are magnified and monstrous, its urgency would not be stilled.

Among the many things clamouring for attention in his scanty leisure time were repairs to the vicarage and the little nearby church.

The slogan 'do it yourself' was unknown in the Lofoten of that time but 'do it yourself' you did—or the job remained undone!

In so poor a parish no funds were available for such matters; any materials needed had to be coaxed from reluctant parishioners who could ill afford them; who looked dourly, almost with suspicion, at what they considered an over-fastidious and inexperienced young man, and who thought the church, and certainly the vicarage, quite good enough as they were.

A few lent their time and their hands, but there were not many volunteers and most days the vicar was to be seen sawing and hammering away by himself.

A few years later when it became necessary to build a new church, though the poverty was no less, there was no lack of helpers. The vicar had become a trusted and well-loved member of the community, and it is recorded that Fru Egede provided food and drink for the workmen 'in a manner which showed her practical sense and kindly heart'; while the versatile vicar, exchanging hammer for brush, painted—or re-painted, opinions differ—the church's altarpiece. But now, for the most part, he laboured alone.

It had been pleasant, if hard, work in the long-lighted summer days when the sun never quite touched the horizon but before midnight was climbing upward for another day, and people were already going about their business at two and three o'clock in the morning.

He had been anxious that the work should be completed before the winter—reported to be harsher here than on Hinnöy—set in. Now everything was nearly finished. Roofs no longer leaked, and the wind would find fewer cracks to whistle through in the warped wooden walls.

By the first day of November all was done: and none too soon.

Winter set in early, harsh indeed! Mountainous seas crashed on the rocks; gales of hurricane force screamed over the islands. There was

> '. . . lightning and the thunder's roar
> Snow, rain and hail, and storm implacable . . .'

Hardships of all kinds gripped the islands. Boats and fishing gear, however carefully protected, were damaged or washed away. On the more distant islands, where for some weeks it was impossible for boats to take food, there was actual starvation. The vicar had plenty to do—and to think about—but the Voice still troubled him . . .

By now Fru Egede knew her husband's secret. She sympathised with his desire to help a neglected people; she thought long and carefully about the matter, and finally succeeded in convincing herself it was not only a foolhardy, but a wildly impossible scheme. And she made every effort to discourage it! Where, she asked, was the money to come from to finance such an enterprise? Were they not almost in debt now on their miserable salary? And even were money forthcoming, how could they reach such a distant country—much less live in it, since it was almost entirely covered in ice and snow, and inhabited by savages?

These things, she insisted, she *knew*; she remembered hearing them when a child from her brother Niels in Bergen who had sailed there on a whaler. And another thing, she continued, how did Hans know the voice he heard was not the voice of the devil tempting him—the lure of pride—that deadliest of all the seven deadly sins against which he was for ever preaching and admonishing others?

The truth was, even though she herself did not perhaps fully realise it, Gertrud Egede was afraid; afraid that this impetuous young husband of hers would exchange substance for shadow; drag her from loved and familiar surroundings to danger and discomfort—possibly even death.

28

Deep in her heart she knew well enough there was no temptation of the devil about it; men linked with evil do not look as her husband had looked that golden October evening . . .

It is often said there is no gainsaying the will of God. Far from succeeding in discouraging her husband in his 'hazardous enterprise' as it later came to be called, Fru Egede had actually helped him achieve it! For greatly to her dismay, he simply brushed aside the question of money; of transport; of ice and snow and savages—even the devil, and pounced on the fact that away in Bergen was someone—not even a stranger but a member of his own family—who had actually visited Greenland! And as soon as he had a spare moment he shut himself in his study and sat scratching away with a worn quill-pen, finally emerging with a thick letter in his hand. It was to Niels Rasch at Bergen begging for every available scrap of information about Greenland he and his friends could supply.

The first step in the long campaign ahead had been taken.

It took a long time in those days for a letter to reach Bergen and an answer to be received in reply, but the busiest season of the year was at hand and there was little time for thinking about personal affairs. Very soon the great fishing fleet would put to sea for its annual harvest; every able-bodied man, woman and child in the islands was needed to help in some way. During the time the men were away at sea, there were their families to care for, and when at last the fleet returned with its splendid catch—it was almost a record year—there was the unloading, the cleaning, and the hanging of the fish on the great racks to dry—work in which all took part.

It was almost autumn before a reply came in answer to the letter to Bergen. But before Hans had leisure to consider it and decide what step to take next, he was caught up in a new and wonderful experience. Early in October his first child was born; a boy—a strong and happy baby. They crhistened him Paul.

What step to take next? Niels Rasch had written—and his letter reveals something of the confusion and inaccuracy of the maps of the time—that 'the land now called Greenland should rightly bear the name of Spitzbergen . . . there are no human beings to be seen there, but in Greenland, towards the south, there are savages'. And he went on to say that the eastern side 'where in

29

former times Norsemen are said to have lived, cannot now be explored because of the drift-ice blocking the coast'.

To his eager, impatient brother-in-law the letter was not particularly helpful. Hans was worried and despondent. The statement about the ice-blocked eastern coast 'where Norsemen were said to have lived' particularly disturbed him. The Voice within left him no peace, and he writes in his diary that time passed for him 'in great doubt and disturbance of mind'.

The long winter wore away; the spring came; his baby son grew and thrived and was a constant delight. But for Hans all happiness was overshadowed by the insistence of the Voice within him.

'Early in the summer', he writes in his diary, 'after much thought and prayer', he decided on a plan of action. This was nothing less than the drafting of a letter to the King—a very daring matter in those days for a young, poor, and totally unknown clergyman in a remote province.

This letter, or memorial as it was called, written in the stilted formal language of the time, put forward what was described as a 'proposal', namely the 'conversion and enlightenment of the Greenlanders, based upon Scriptures exhorting Christians to carry out missionary work among the heathen'.

It was despatched, not direct to the King, not even to Hans' own Bishop in Trondheim, but to the Bishop of Bergen—Bergen being the port from which any ship for Greenland would sail, with a letter humbly begging him to forward it 'to those in power'.

The Bishop replied kindly. But while he commended the 'proposal', he disapproved its writer's desire to give up his parish in order to preach to the heathen 'for', as he pointed out, 'this could bear little fruit seeing that Hans Egede lacked any knowledge of their barbaric tongue'.

However, he was sufficiently in sympathy with the matter to agree to forward the letter to the church authorities in Copenhagen 'in order that it might be laid before the King'.

Hans was overjoyed! His spirits soared and he had further cause for happiness; by the time autumn came again, a little less than a year after the birth of Paul, another son was born.

He was christened Niels—after his sailor uncle in Bergen.

All too soon much of this happiness was shattered. The letter to the Bishop of Bergen brought an unlooked-for sequel. From the Bishop himself or from his household rumours of Hans Egede's 'hazardous enterprise' as it was described, spread through Bergen. As a result more letters descended on the Vaagan vicarage in a month than would normally have come in a year.

Friends of Hans, relatives of his wife, wrote furiously denouncing such rashness—nay, presumption! Letters reviling and condemning Hans were received by Fru Egede's mother who accused him of deliberately setting out to bring ruin and misery to his wife and children. In her anxiety she even tried to set her daughter against what she considered her monster of a husband! Poor Fru Egede, exhausted with the care of a new baby and the barely year-old, but already adventurous Paul, was on the verge of being driven to regret her marriage.

To allow such domestic strife to continue was impossible. It was not only unbearable but unchristian. That Hans dealt firmly with his mother-in-law is probable though not recorded, but he writes in his diary of a decision to make his wife see his resolve 'as truly the will of God; that it was our bounden duty to show a resolute self-denial by leaving our home and going forth to preach the gospel among the heathen'.

Later he records, 'we both laid the matter before God in prayer and the answer was the bending of her will so that she confidently promised to follow me wherever I went, like a true Sara, thus strengthening my will to persevere'.

Indeed from now on it was Fru Egede who, temptation by the devil and interference by her mother disposed of, became the leading spirit in the 'hazardous enterprise'. So much so that when in later years, worn out with worry, opposition and constant frustration, her husband was almost prepared to abandon it, it was she who insisted there was now no turning back.

'By her faith and constancy I cannot say how much she encouraged me', wrote Hans. 'She, a frail woman, showed greater faith and manliness than I!'

There was already war between the joint kingdoms of Norway and Denmark against Sweden; now, to make matters worse, plague broke out in Copenhagen.

These calamities overshadowed everything else. All communication with court and church affairs in Denmark became increasingly difficult. At the end of the year, nothing further having come of his 'proposal' Hans sent a copy of it to his friend the Bishop of Trondheim.

The Bishop was an old man and his geography appears to have been curiously hazy. He apparently believed Greenland to be part of America 'not far from Cuba'. He offered one or two quite impractical suggestions, but declared the project was justified and he himself 'willing to assist by word and deed'.

His letter, while it made Hans no wiser, gave him a little hope and greatly increased his confidence. So much so that he wrote another and more detailed 'proposal' to the King. In this he boldly points out that 'all Christians have a duty towards missions so long as any heathens exist' and 'such duty rests specially with the government and teachers of the people. The church', he continues, 'must not be confined to one spot but a vessel carried from one place to another. God moves the candle-stick from where no work is done and Christians will be called severely to account if they content themselves merely in trading with the heathen'.

To whom this bravely worded document was sent is not clear—certainly not direct to the King, though it is known to have been discussed by his council in January 1712. In January 1713—two days short of a year—it was forwarded to the church authorities. Here 'the poor but zealous vicar's letter' was recommended for special consideration in the hope that one day something might come of it 'when time and opportunity offered'.

To the Vaagan vicarage however, came only a melancholy message to have patience; not until there was some improvement in the present difficult times could it be expected such a matter would be considered at court.

'In this way', wrote Hans in deep depression, 'my commendable enterprise was put off year after year', and he adds that his unhappiness was increased by 'obstacles and objections of all kinds' put in his way 'both by friends and by enemies.'

Frustrated and worried, opposed by friends and foes alike, his country at war, no longer a very young man, he still clung grimly to his purpose. A Voice had spoken. . . . But as he went about his daily work or stood gazing seawards in the direction of the land to which his heart was already given, Hans Egede may well have echoed the cry of the psalmist, 'How long, oh Lord, how long?'

Paul and Niels were now nearly five and four years old—strong sturdy little boys, and in the late summer of 1714 their first sister was born.

Both Fru Egede and her husband were delighted with their little daughter, from the beginning a placid, good-tempered baby. They christened her Kirsten after Hans' own sister.

Niels at first had been a little jealous of this small newcomer who absorbed so much of his mother's attention, though when he discovered she could neither walk nor talk but 'only', as he said, 'wail and mew like a sea-bird', while he, Niels, could run and climb and tie knots and fish, his jealousy was short-lived. Very soon he began to love the odd little bundle of clothes—and Lofoten babies of those days were indeed bundles of clothes—layer upon layer of them—that gazed solemnly up at him from her cradle. He would hunt about on the beach for the delicate green and mauve-patterned shells of sea-urchins—so miraculously washed up unbroken on that rocky coast. These he brought home and presented with pride—much offended when Fru Egede complained that they smelt—as they frequently did.

The following year short daily lessons with their father began for both boys.

Paul took more kindly to these than Niels. He soon learnt to read quite well, and he loved drawing. In the long dark winter when so much time had to be spent indoors he would sit for hours covering any paper he could lay hands on with ships and flowers, animals or fishes, frequently digging holes in the paper in his anxiety to make whatever he was trying to draw 'come right'. All too often, as every artist knows, it would only 'come' wrong. Then there were sometimes tears and a furious flinging of the paper on the floor and Paul would change to reading for a time. But not for long; very soon paper and pencil would appear again.

Niels was very much an outdoor boy. He hated to be under a roof of any kind however bad the weather, and when he grew older was given to sneaking out in temperatures well below zero; especially if the Aurora was giving a particularly good display! He cared little for lessons unless it were lessons in splicing ropes, tying knots, or the best way to bait a hook. He and Paul spent many hours watching, imitating—and bothering—the fishermen, and there were few days snow, rain, or sun that they did not play with the fishermen's children on the small sandy beaches near their home.

Pirate and Viking games were the favourites. England was frequently invaded, and 'taken'. Girls were seldom, and grudgingly, allowed to join in, and then only as housewives or hostages, rôles which usually meant sitting about on a distant rock waiting to be rescued or ransomed.

Almost as soon as she could toddle Kirsten was expected to

endure this fate. Sometimes she did, but sometimes there were tears. More often she evaded it by quite simply refusing to stay put, clambering homewards over the slippery boulders bleating plaintively 'like a young seal' as Paul remarked, for her mother.

On one of the sandy beaches where some of the big boulders had rolled down from the cliff above, was a great squarish one that had wedged itself between two ridges of rock. On three sides it had withstood the original crash but on the fourth it had split, cracked, and gradually crumbled away leaving a great gaping hole. The constant washing in and out of the tide had worn this away still more so that now a small smooth-walled cave

34

about four feet square had been formed. Thick, slimy, yellow sea-weed of the sort that pops when you walk on it covered the lower part of all the rocks, and on some of them another kind grew as well. Long, thin and ropey, rather like leather shoe-laces, it grew particularly well on the big fallen boulder, hanging over it like a bead curtain and completely concealing the entrance to the little cave. As the tide came in, gradually submerging the boulder, the curtain of weed could be seen floating outstretched around it, but as the water rose higher it too was covered and nothing marked the place. At low tide, unless you had been told of it or explored very carefully, you would never know of the cave's existence.

It was the perfect hiding place; planning place; and place to be alone.

Sometimes, when she grew older, the boys at their lessons, Kirsten went with her mother to play on the beach. While Fru Egede sat knitting Kirsten, clutching two battered wooden dolls that had once belonged to her mother, would crawl inside the cave, and a doll propped up on either side of her sit gazing, unseen but all-seeing, through the sea-weed curtain at the distant islands and the fleets of little eider-ducks swimming serene and unaware among the near-by skerries.

She loved the dolls' house as she called it, and went with Niels to say good-bye to it before they left Lofoten. She did not cry, but the leaving of it was a lasting hurt.

For a long time she thought of it every day. And she remembered it always.

Like nearly all Norwegian children, Paul and Niels were almost as much at home in a boat as on land, and as they grew older what they loved most was to go with their father when he visited the out-lying islands.

This, however, was a rare delight. For one thing it was a whole day's outing, and a long day at that; an early start and a late return.

Their father sometimes went alone or with the fishermen on grey or doubtful days. If he took the children it had to be the right kind of day—and with some promise of remaining so, for weather in Lofoten can change rapidly and quite unpredictably, and a trip started on a smooth blue sea may well end in a return soaked with rain and drenched with spray.

To Fru Egede these outings were always an anxiety, and how-

35

ever busy she might be she would make constant journeys to the cliff-top near the house about the time the travellers might be expected home and run down to the beach waving a welcome as soon as they were sighted.

Sailing between the islands and the dozens of skerries around them was an enchantment: blue and mysterious on the horizon, they rose grey and precipitous as you neared them. It looked almost impossible to land but always, hidden away in at least one sheltered place was a tiny harbour; a few scattered cottages with flowers growing gaily on their turfed roofs; perhaps a small farm, and—everywhere—cod-racks!

On the smaller and more distant islands the grey-black cliffs seemed to rise almost sheer from the sea and to be covered, tier upon tier, with what looked like the small pointed shapes of crocus flowers.

At a signal from their father Paul and Niels would clap their hands and shout and the white shapes immediately rose high in the air revealing themselves as myriads and myriads of sea-birds. Calling and mewing to each other they sailed and circled over-head, dark or silver-bright as they wheeled about, now facing, now against the sun, weaving a garland in the blue and cloudless northern sky. Sometimes they flew so high they were almost invisible; sometimes they went swooping by so low you could see their little yellow legs and feet lying neatly side by side, stretched out along their bodies—almost transparent against the light, and the dazzling white underfeathers of their small fan-like tails. Once Niels had tried to grab one as it flew past, nearly upsetting the boat as a result. He had paid heavily for that! Hans Egede loved his children deeply but like many other parents of that time he was no sparer of the rod. In his opinion a boy could not learn early enough the way to behave, or not behave, in a boat.

Perhaps it was a valuable lesson. Years later, learning the exacting discipline required for the management of that most difficult of small craft, the kayak, Niels sometimes remembered that day. At the time, however, it had been a bitter experience. A holiday begun with a beating does not augur well!

But if Hans Egede did not believe in sparing the rod he also followed the Bible in not letting the sun go down on his wrath. Always, in a few hours, all was forgotten and forgiven and usually not referred to again, and this particular day had ended happily.

Before they were seven-years-old Paul and Niels had had their first lessons in rowing. Two years later when they left Lofoten for Bergen both boys could handle a boat as well, if not better, than many a grown-up.

It was early in the summer of 1716 that the great decision to go to Bergen had originally been taken. For over six long years—and very long they seemed—Hans Egede had tried, and tried and tried again, and he seemed as far from realising his 'hazardous enterprise' as when he started.

The war showed no sign of ending; his letters and 'proposals' still lay unheeded, gathering dust away in Copenhagen, and so, he was convinced, they would continue to lie. If, he reasoned, he went to Bergen, he could at least collect information about Greenland from whaling skippers and others who had sailed there, and try and interest people in the matter. From Bergen too, it might be possible to go to Copenhagen and perhaps even make an attempt to secure an audience with the King and so put the matter before him personally.

37

It was a bold scheme, the last desperate hope of a brave but discouraged man.

The decision taken, Hans wrote to his Bishop for permission to resign his living. In due course the permission was granted.

But Hans Egede did not leave Lofoten; no successor could be found who would accept so poor a living!

All through these last bitter years, true to her promise, Fru Egede had cheered and encouraged her husband; helped with every plan, upheld his views to those who opposed them. Now, when this last blow fell, all the more shattering because wholly unexpected, and so crushing him that he seemed almost prepared to abandon his idea, it was she who insisted there was now no turning back. A successor would be found; to Bergen they would go.

The year had been a hard one; the war dragged on; a poor fishing season was followed by a bad local harvest while corn, which always had to come from the south, was difficult to obtain and prohibitive in price.

There was trouble and distress throughout the islands. Engulfed in the clouds of misery all about them, harassed by their own uncertainties, it was often difficult to keep cheerful, and the happiness brought by the birth of another little daughter was doubly welcome.

Unlike Niels of herself, Kirsten was not jealous of the new baby though it was a long time before she learnt to pronounce her name—Petronella—correctly.

The new year came; peace seemed no nearer, and Hans wrote again to his bishop definitely resigning his living. Whether he waited until a successor was found is not known, but it is possible, for it was not until July in the following year that the Egede family finally left for Bergen.

On his last Sunday in the islands, Hans preached his farewell sermon, choosing for his text words from St. Paul's Epistle to the Corinthians . . . 'for we have hope . . . to preach the gospel in lands beyond you'.

The little wooden church which he had helped to build was filled to overflowing; there was not a spare inch of room! The islanders sat squashed against each other in the utmost discomfort. Those who could not get in stood wedged together in the porch, the door of which was left open so that others standing outside in the churchyard, could, by straining their ears, hear their vicar for the last time, while some of the younger and more agile climbed up and perched themselves precariously on the high window-sills.

In those days of very long sermons it was expected today's would be long indeed, but Hans had never spoken more briefly. Immediately below him sat Fru Egede, the sleeping Petronella in her arms. On one side, snuggled close against her was Kirsten, gazing upward with round blue eyes at her father strange to her in his long, black gown, and white frilled ruff; on the other Paul and Niels. Both boys were on their very best behaviour; no whispering; no turning round to see who was behind, but sitting quietly and listening attentively.

As he preached, Hans glanced once or twice at the little group beneath him and when he had finshed his sermon, instead of leaving the pulpit, he stood in silence for a moment looking down on them. Then, turning to the congregation, he asked for their prayers, not only for the work to which he had set his hand, but for his courageous wife, and for his young family.

Two days later, with all their meagre possessions, and something evidently very precious, strongly corded in a wooden box and carried carefully by Hans himself, the family sailed for Svolvær.

It was not until they had all said goodbye to the crowds that gathered there to see them off, and, showered with small gifts, were finally aboard the schooner that was to take them to Bergen that Hans revealed what the wooden box contained. Standing beside the rail of the ship, he carefully uncorded it and drew out a large lidded, silver tankard. It had been given to Fru Egede and himself three years before, a present from the islanders in gratitude for kindness to them and their families, and in memory of the record fishing season of 1715. Round the lid was the date— '9th February, anno. 1715' and a reference to 'golden fisheries out of which silver mugs are created'.

Hans stood holding it up for all to see. It was a gesture he knew would be understood; a bond between them. Wherever he went the silver tankard would go too and with it, not only the memory of Lofoten's 'golden fisheries' but of Lofoten's men, women and children.

He was still holding it when the schooner weighed anchor and sailed slowly out of the harbour.

The silver tankard journeyed far, and can be seen in Denmark today at Frederiksborg Museum near Copenhagen, little the worse for its long travels.

5

On Board—and Overboard

PART ONE

The long journey to Bergen was an exciting time for the four Egede children.

If Fru Egede had hoped for a little rest and peace after the packing up and departure from Lofoten she was disappointed. To keep the boys—and often Kirsten as well—from poking into every corner of the ship; from climbing on the rails and falling over or even through them, kept her fully occupied. Even Petronella who had barely learnt to walk, would escape from her mother whenever she could and try to toddle after them.

Hans Egede liked his children to be adventurous and enquiring and he realised the fascination the ship held for them but, as has already been said, he was a stern disciplinarian. For the first day or two there were some other boys on board, a little older than the Egede children. Their companionship seemed to go to the heads of Paul and Niels who became wild and unmanageable— once or twice what was described as 'flagrantly disobedient'.

On the evening of the third day at sea Hans called his sons to him and announced that from tomorrow lessons would take place every morning as at home; and Kirsten must start to learn her alphabet. And—he held up a warning finger—permission to roam over the ship must be sought—and from the Captain himself.

Paul and Niels, who had expected the voyage to be one long glorious holiday, were disgusted! The thought of sitting confined in the tiny stuffy little cabin they shared with their father, or in the ship's small and almost as stuffy saloon missing all the excitements of the arrival and departure from the little ports at which the ship stopped so often, was torture. As for asking anything of the Captain—a great Viking of a man—six feet six inches tall, broad in proportion, with piercing blue eyes—the very thought appalled them! But Hans was adamant. Next morning, out came the lesson books and in a corner of the stuffy little saloon they

41

sat; one hour for Kirsten, two hours for the boys—surely the longest hours anyone had ever known?

Throughout her life Kirsten was to remember her learning of the alphabet—three letters longer than our English one. The big and little twin A's; the strange Æ; the A leaning against an E as if it were tired; the ø with the line through its middle. . . . Before they reached Bergen she knew it all perfectly.

Her father was delighted with her quickness.

'Before we sail for Greenland', he told her, thinking rather in terms of months than of years, 'you will be able to read!'

Sometimes Hans relaxed his stern rule. Whenever anything of special interest was to be seen lesson time was shortened or even abandoned. Crossing the arctic circle was one of these occasions.

It was a glorious day. A misty haze lay on the horizon so that sea and sky seemed one in their blueness. Even so, and although it was now August, snow still lay about the jagged mountain tops and the slight breeze from the land was cold—chilled by the breath of a great glacier lying near.

Everyone crowded on deck; even the Viking captain left the bridge and talked with his passengers. Niels lurking as near as he dared to the great man heard something which interested him very much. The captain was joking with some men; asking if they knew the old saying that he who has crossed the equator may put one foot on the table after supper but he who has crossed the arctic circle may put both feet?

Both feet on the table! It sounded the very essence of independence and grown-up-ness! Niels could hardly wait for supper time; it was a long way off and he had difficulty in keeping his information to himself. But at last it came and as the meal ended he looked eagerly about him, fully expecting to see all the men loll back in their chairs, bring out their pipes or snuff boxes, and take advantage of this wonderful privilege. But—nobody did! Could they have forgotten? He waited a moment or two longer and decided that, incredibly, they had. Then he, Niels, would remind them! And wriggling about in the rather confined space allotted him at the table, he managed to put his feet in their none-too-clean shoes on the still spotless tablecloth, and folding his arms and half-closing his eyes, leant back with an air of great satisfaction.

His parents were engaged in conversation with other passengers and for a moment Niels remained unnoticed; but when he was—!

Fru Egede was almost too scandalised to speak! Kirsten's eyes were as round as the o's in the alphabet. Paul looked half envious, half disapproving. As for Hans, his quick temper was roused—almost to violence. Striding across the narrow little saloon he seized Niels by his coat collar, jerked him to his feet and shook him soundly! What scandalous, *atrocious* behaviour was this! And he threatened him with the worst beating of his life.

Half-choked with the shaking he was getting, Niels tried to explain, but before he had got further than, 'the captain . . . the captain said . . .' the captain himself was beside them.

His great bulk seemed to fill the whole saloon. Even Hans Egede, who was a tall man, looked small beside him.

'One moment, Vicar; one moment', he said and he laid a huge and restraining hand on Hans' arm.

'The boy is exercising an old privilege, I think—and at my suggestion, I fear! I noticed him listening very intently to some of my conversation this morning. Isn't that so, boy?' and he turned to Niels.

'But I said men, my son', he went on, not waiting for an answer, '*men*—how old are you?'

'Eight—*nearly* . . . Eight-in-November, sir', gasped Niels, the breath almost shaken out of him.

'Let him go sir', said the captain to Hans. 'Did you not know the saying—you've crossed before?'

'Yes', Hans admitted, his fiery temper quickly evaporating, yes, he did, though he had forgotten it.

'Go to your mother—she calls', he said, releasing his hold on his son's collar.

Niels squirmed under the table and came up on the other side; it seemed much the simplest—and quickest—way. Hans looked rather disconcerted but the captain roared with laughter and winked at Niels with one of his bright blue eyes.

'That's a good boy of yours, Vicar!' he said when Niels had gone away with Fru Egede. A remark Paul found somewhat puzzling.

From then on, however, neither he nor Niels had any fear of the captain and there were many escorted trips to all parts of the ship. There was even a glorious half-hour on the bridge when they were each allowed to take a turn at the wheel and steer. By the time they reached Bergen they considered that there was nothing about a schooner they did not know.

They were ready to sail not only to Greenland but round the world!

On Kirsten's birthday, August 13th, they reached Trondheim where the ship stayed nearly a whole day and everyone went ashore.

This was an adventure indeed! Trondheim, once the capital of Norway, was still an important centre of trade, the home of her greatest cathedral, and of many rich men, officials and merchants.

Not even Fru Egede had seen so large a town, such houses and shops! They walked up the narrow, dusty streets from the harbour and turned into the wide cobbled ones, marvelling at the big white-painted timber houses decorated with carvings, flights of stone steps with beautiful wrought-iron railings on either side leading to their tall brass-studded front doors; at the ladies in silk dresses, and the gentlemen in velvet coats strolling about. As for the shops with their splendid array of iron and silver ware, glass and pottery, fine leather and rich furs, they seemed hardly real. The market place was gay with flowers they had never seen, fruit and vegetables they had never eaten. It was like living in a fairy tale! Finally they turned into a long, wide, tree-lined street and there at the far end stood the great cathedral,* tall, grey, majestic, its massive square tower rising almost as high as the tallest trees!

To the Egede children who had never seen a stone building larger than a big stable it seemed impossible that so many stones could lie one upon another in safety; the tall tower not shake and fall as the churches and fortresses they tried to build with stones on the shore at Lofoten always did.

Inside the cathedral seemed even taller; dark, solemn, immense; lit only by great windows of coloured glass. Coming in from the darkness outside it was hard to see, but their eyes soon became accustomed to the sombre light. They stood gazing at the giant pillars, at the dazzling glass, and away towards the altar where a semi-circle of high-backed chairs covered in tooled and painted leather stood on either side of the great gilded throne where the Kings of Norway were crowned.

Hans would like to have seen his old friend the bishop whose

---

* In 1718 Trondheim Cathedral was being partly rebuilt after a bad fire, but the tower, east end, and part of the nave were undamaged and would have looked much as described. A spire was added at a later date.

palace stood close to the cathedral but the bishop, he was told, was away. He had gone to take confirmation services in his scattered diocese, and was not expected home for some weeks.

On the way back they passed through the market place again and because it was Kirsten's birthday her father stopped at a gingerbread stall and bought some.

The gingerbread was cut into shapes; hearts, stars, and some crude attempts at animals. Hans gave each child a piece; even Petronella beaming in her mother's arms clutched something faintly resembling a seal in a small fat hand.

It seemed a very long way back to the ship and before they were half way there Kirsten found it hard to keep up with the others. She kept reminding herself she was four years old now but she fell behind so often that at last Hans went back for her, swung her up on his shoulder and carried her the rest of the way.

The weather, which had been almost perfect all the way from Lofoten—warm, sunny, but with enough breeze to keep the ship moving swiftly, continued to be fair. The day after leaving Trondheim there was a stretch of open sea unsheltered by islands and skerries to be crossed. In bad weather it was often rough here and seasoned travellers went below and stayed there. Even in good weather the great Atlantic rollers sometimes caused the ship to pitch and roll unhappily.

Hans sent the children and their mother below but stayed on deck himself. He was a good sailor, never sea-sick, and preferred being in the open air.

The ship was already beginning to roll a little and he stood leaning against the rail in conversation with another passenger. They were discussing the flight and habits of the sea-birds that followed the ship so persistently—hopeful of scraps from the cook's galley; noting the difference in their markings and the amazing fact that no two birds were alike. Hans' attention was caught by a one-legged herring-gull—a young bird still in its brown-mottled plumage—and the valiant manner in which it kept up with the other birds. Pointing it out to his companion he leant out over the rail to observe it better. The ship gave a sudden lurch. Hans was jerked forward and lost his hold. Before he could recover it she rolled badly, and he fell over into the sea.

His fellow passenger lost no time and his cry, 'Man overboard!'

echoed over the ship. Ropes were thrown, the ship hove to; orders given to lower a boat . . .

Down in the cabin Fru Egede heard the alarming cry, 'Man overboard', and felt the slowing of the ship . . . One of the seamen she supposed . . . and hushing the frightened children she prayed silently but passionately for his safety.

Hans was a good swimmer but the ship was already many yards off and still moving away from him. He saw one of the ropes that had been thrown and struck out towards it. But Atlantic rollers are strong and the water, even in summer in those latitudes, very cold. In less than five minutes he felt cramp attack first one foot . . . then the other . . . spread up his legs. The rope, floating in the trough of a roller, was no longer visible. . . . The cramp increased . . . became acute. . . .

The rope re-appeared for a moment, but it was no nearer and in that moment Hans realised he could never reach it.

Less than a second later he heard a shout and a rope hit the water beside him. He seized and clung to it, and looking behind him saw the hull of a fishing smack and the anxious faces of two men . . .

With difficulty he was pulled aboard the little, rocking boat, and blue with cold, wrapped in one of the fishermen's coats, was rowed back to the ship. She had stopped and they were lowering a boat.

Hans was none the worse for his ordeal but he knew he had never been nearer death. He regarded his rescue as a sign from Heaven; a proof that his life had been spared for some good purpose.

More than ever he was convinced he had some mission—some special task to fulfil.

6

To Greenland's Icy Mountains

PART ONE

Bergen, often said to be one of the wettest cities in Europe, was
not living up to its reputation on the day the Egede family arrived
there. Under a cloudless blue sky, every rail and plank scrubbed,
every bit of brass polished and shining, the ship sailed slowly past
the dozens of little islands and skerries guarding the approach
to the town's magnificent harbour. To Paul and Niels, watching
from the deck, it looked even more exciting than Trondheim!

The schooner anchored near the great stone fortress known as
Haakon's Hall—so near that they could see the soldiers with
their muskets pacing to and fro on guard.

While the ship was being made fast they stood gazing around
them in wonder. At the great fortress; at the tall wooden, sharply
pointed gabled houses that lined the wharf—the homes, counting-
houses and store rooms of rich merchants and shipowners; at the
shipping in the harbour. Never, even when the whole Lofoten
fishing fleet was mustered in the spring, had they seen so many
ships together! Big ships, little ships; every kind from fishing
smacks and great full-rigged four-masters, twice—three times—
the size of the schooner on which they stood; foreign voices called
from their decks; unknown flags flew at their mastheads.

Away beyond them, under the high hills which rose sharply
up from the harbour on three sides, buildings seemed to stretch
for ever. The sun shone on tall towers, on gilded crosses and
weather-cocks. On the wharf below, sailors shouted; citizens
cheered and waved. It was all very gay!

From the moment he set foot in Bergen—or so it seemed to
Hans Egede—everyone he met appeared to know about his plans.

This may have been partly due to his brother-in-law Niels
Rasch at whose house the family probably stayed, and partly
to friends and other relatives living in the town. While some
approved these plans and regarded Hans with amazement, even

47

awe—a sort of super-man—others condemned them outright and he himself as fanatical, if not actually mad.

Used by now to hostility, Hans paid little attention to any of them and encouraged by the few who supported him, lost no time in setting about his plan of campaign. This was to call on the most important men in the town, put his case clearly before them, and plead for their assistance in carrying it out. When enough citizens had promised support, he would go to Copenhagen, try to obtain an audience with the King and ask for his patronage and help.

Bergen's leading citizens, for the most part merchants and shipowners, regarded Hans and his proposals much as his own and his brother-in-law's friends had done.

'Some', he writes, 'judged them in a Christian manner'; others, while they commended him personally, would give only the most cautious answers. *If* peace was restored, *if* the King would support the undertaking, they *might* be prepared to send ships to Greenland. . . But the majority roundly and bluntly condemned both plans and planner as dangerous and foolhardy in the extreme.

On one point, however, they were all agreed, so long as the war continued, and difficulty of communication persisted, nothing could be done.

Once again Hans resigned himself to waiting. This time he was less discouraged. Change of scene, meeting new people, had helped to raise his spirits. There was hope in the air too; signs that the war was definitely ending. With renewed zeal he set to work again.

This time his pleadings took the form of a letter. It was dated November 26th, 1718, and addressed 'to all lovers of Jesus Christ . . . high and low . . . inhabitants and citizens of mark within the city . . .'

After pointing out that no people had a better right to go to Greenland than Norwegians since it was originally colonised by them, he mentions the tempting possibility of finding 'rich mines and minerals', and sets out detailed suggestions as to how the expedition should be organised. A friend from the north has already promised 1,000 rigsdaler (about £200—a large sum in those days), and he himself, 'in spite of opposition from friends and relations—even at first from his own wife, has given up his livelihood for what he believes to be a divine call.' Quoting from the Bible in support of preaching the gospel to heathens, he

48

Anniversary stamp issued in 1958 to commemorate the bi-centenary of Hans Egede's death.

Hans Egede and his wife—carving outside the Nicolai church, Copenhagen.

Godthaab—showing statue of Hans Egede and the hospital on the left; the church and the settlement house on the right. *(by Mogens Lindhard)*

The settlement house at Godthaab. The house is exactly as it was built, with the exception of the sun-porch.

ends by saying he is already preparing to journey to Copenhagen to ask the King for his patronage and support.

On November 30th, exactly four days after the letter was written, the Swedish King, Charles XII, died. This brought a turning-point in the war, hopes of its speedy end and the declaration of peace.

Hans was ready to start for Copenhagen at the first possible moment, but—as usual—he had to wait!

Never the kind of man who could be idle, he busied himself with various occupations and skills which he felt would be of use to him in the far-off land which he was so determined to reach. Among other things he took lessons in chemistry and surveying, he also seized every opportunity he could to talk with skippers and owners of whaling ships who had sailed to or near the Greenland coast.

The most helpful of these men was Hans Mathias, a Dane who had come to Bergen as a young man and, with others, engaged in the whaling trade around Spitzbergen. From as early as 1707 he and his partner Von Bärenfels had sent ships through Davis Strait on whaling expeditions up the west coast of Greenland.

'In order,' as he told Hans, 'that the trade should not be entirely in the hands of the Dutch seeing that the country originally belonged to Norsemen!'

The loss of two ships in 1714 had discouraged him from continuing, but he was able to tell Hans many important things such as the position of possible harbours; about the climate, the soil, the fishing, and other vital matters.

Both men were to prove good friends for when at long last the fitting out of an expedition had become a possibility and its fate hung in the balance, the fact that they, with their first-hand experience spoke in support of it may well have tilted the scales in its favour.

But this was not yet; almost another two years of waiting lay ahead; long, weary months of frustration; of hopes raised only to be disappointed.

As expected, the war now came quickly to an end and though the peace was not signed, travel between Bergen and Copenhagen became easier. Even so it was not until the spring of 1719 that Hans was able to set off.

Rough and uncomfortable as the journey was he was in high spirits and full of hope. Once he could see the King in person all, he was sure, would be well.

He looked forward too to seeing Copenhagen again, visiting the University and looking up old friends. But he was hardly off the ship before he found disappointment waiting for him. The King was away—and not expected back in the city for some weeks. Once again Hans had to wait. But now he did not grudge the time for he had more than enough to do.

Among the few who had always encouraged and supported his plans was Thomas von Westen, the first missionary to Lapland.

For a long time he and Hans had been corresponding. No one knew better the difficulties of travelling with no reliable maps in an almost unknown country, and of trying to teach and preach in an almost unknown tongue. He wrote now to tell Hans about various maps and a detailed history of Greenland; a manuscript that could be seen in the Royal Library in Copenhagen and, what was perhaps equally, if not more important, where a list of many Greenlandic words was to be found.

These words had been written down from the speech of some captive eskimos brought from Greenland by one of the last expeditions to go there. A picture of these men hung in the Royal Museum of Art; four sad-faced prisoners holding spears, bows and arrows, and fish.

Hans stood looking at them for a long time in silence, his heart wrung by the misery in their eyes.

Following Von Westen's advice he found and carefully copied the list of words; made tracings from maps, and read everything he could about Greenland.

As he did so he was often surprised—and disheartened—to learn how many plans and schemes concerning it had got no further than the paper or parchment on which they were written. Particularly interesting was the manuscript mentioned by Von Westen. This, written in Latin, was by an Icelander. Like Hans, he too had known and loved the Sagas from boyhood; he had also had the advantage of being able to collect information from his fellow countrymen.

In Iceland interest in Greenland, so inaccessible and yet so near—on a clear day the mountains behind the impenetrable ice off the east coast, could be seen from high ground in the north—had never died out. There was knowledge of it before, and, perhaps more important, after the days when the great sagas were written. Knowledge handed down from one generation to another through the long dark centuries when few ships sailed the polar seas and the flame of learning burnt low in Europe.

With the manuscript was a detailed plan worked out some years earlier by an Icelander for the re-settlement of Greenland in which the original route taken by Erik-the-Red was to be followed. To this the writer had added suggestions of his own.

As Hans read it seemed to him almost as if he were reading his own words; at times the very sentences he had used in his petition stared at him from the page! 'An advance party . . . establishment of settlements . . . perhaps some soldiery as a precaution in trading . . . possibility of finding precious metals and ores . . .' There were even references to the old Christian settlers 'whose descendants, if found, should be helped . . .'

This plan, he was to learn, had been all but carried out—in 1705. Why the expedition never sailed now seems to be unknown but it is certain King Frederik IV, who had given his consent to it, had been interested.

This interest was revived when he received the fervent petition Hans now composed, and with various testimonials, including one from his parishioners in Lofoten 'testifying to his good conduct in his office', sent to the newly established Missionary College to be forwarded. As a result, when he at last attained his audience with the King he was not only graciously, but enthusiastically received.

There is no doubt Frederik IV liked and admired Hans Egede and that he himself was a man after Hans' own heart; in his letters and diaries he frequently mentions the King's 'unvarying kindness' to him. The two men had many interests in common—not least their religious faith. It was this King, as Hans had been careful to point out in his petition, who had sent the first Danish missionaries to the East Indies, whose departure he himself had witnessed when a student at the University.

But though personally enthusiastic, the King, like many another monarch, was largely bound by the advice of his ministers.

He promised, however, to have the matter discussed at his next council meeting, and to do all he could to further the proposal.

Full of hope, Hans returned to Bergen.

The meeting of the King and his ministers did not take place until November and was a stormy one. The question of Hans Egede and his proposed expedition called forth long and bitter arguments and there was violent disagreement. Finally it was proposed to call a meeting of the chief merchants and councillors in Bergen to decide whether they considered 'trade with Greenland could be carried on with advantage'.

The King gave his assent and a meeting was arranged to take place in Bergen the following week.

PART TWO

On the appointed day, as Hans walked to the Town Hall through the narrow cobbled streets in the cold, wet, November gloom, he felt strangely apprehensive. This, he was sure, would be a vital meeting; today his fate—and the fate of the country he so longed to serve, decided. No inner Voice spoke to him now and he was conscious only of his long struggle; of eleven years of striving and pleading, of hostility and indifference—and of so little encouragement.

But little as it was he clung to it, and rebuking himself sharply for his lack of courage and faith he stopped and oblivious of the cold rain stood for a moment in prayer. Then squaring his shoulders he went forward to learn his fate.

A large company had assembled in the Town Hall. The leading merchants and ship owners; skippers and mates of whaling ships—anyone of importance who had navigated—or tried to navigate Davis strait, and had set foot on the West Greenland coast.

One after another steely-eyed weather beaten men got to their feet and gave their experiences and their views. Many of the statements conflicted, but all laid stress on the dangers and difficulties of navigation in these waters, and almost all spoke of their voyages with bitterness, even hatred.

The horror of the ice—the great floating bergs that could crush the stoutest ship; the cruel climate—'never fine for more than half a day at a time' as one skipper complained; the blizzards; the bitter winds; and, especially, the penetrating cold of the fogs which descended without warning, adding to every hazard and sometimes lasting for days on end.

One captain spoke of how his ship had been crushed in the ice in a blizzard, boats lowered on to the ice swept away and

52

lost, and how, with other survivors, he had managed to reach land and after several days of wandering found 'dwellings of turf and stone, like those to be seen in Finnmark'. Inside were 'skins, seal blubber, and seal oil'; also 'sea birds eggs and smoked fish of which they ate their fill.' Some natives were seen 'running about on the mountains'.

After two days walking they came to 'a large plain covered with juniper where natives had shot at them with bows and arrows'. They had fled and further north found a Dutch ship which took them on board.

Another skipper said that he had been on four voyages to Greenland. With others he had landed on the west coast and walked some eight to twelve miles inland. Though it was July snow was still on the ground. He saw a herd of reindeer and some deserted huts built of mud and stones; nothing green, not a blade of grass. He ended by saying firmly that so long as God gave him his bread elsewhere he would keep well away from such a land!

Another said that in his opinion Danes and Norwegians could never winter in the country owing to the intense cold. 'Even in summer it was necessary to go about in mittens'.

Hans sat listening as one after another confirmed these gloomy statements or made equally depressing ones; his hopes and strivings being ruthlessly shattered and destroyed.

And then there was a gleam of hope. Von Bärenfels, partner and one-time skipper of Hans Mathias, from both of whom as already mentioned, Hans had received kindness and encouragement, spoke in great detail giving many important facts.

Not only had he sent many ships to Greenland, he said, but for some years had had the idea of founding settlements there. As to Danes and Norwegians being unable to winter in the country, if 'the miserable savages' his men had seen could do so, so could they! There were great rivers full of fish, and in places beautiful green plains with here and there the remains of stone buildings which he was certain were the ruins of the old Christian settlements. As for trading, the natives had been seen to go in large numbers aboard Dutch ships and this, he added amid some laughter, showed very clearly they had something worth having to sell!

He ended by saying he hoped sincerely that God would further Hans Egede's 'noble undertaking'. Had it been ten years earlier when he was a younger man and at the height of his prosperity he would certainly have contributed a considerable sum towards carrying it out.

He was by far the most convincing speaker but no one else, not even his own skippers, showed much enthusiasm, and others who had previously appeared favourably disposed kept silent.

There was no doubt the meeting on the whole was unfavourable.

Hans came sadly away. Why, he asked himself as he walked dejectedly homewards, had those who had previously seemed in favour of his plans not spoken? Fear, he decided was the reason; fear that if they spoke well of the country they would be sent there again, possibly to stay for a time.

The more he thought it over, the more sure of this he became. It was fortunate, he reflected, that he had taken testimonials in support of his plan to Copenhagen. With only the report of this meeting to go on, the King, much less his ministers, might have good reason to suspect they had been told a pack of lies!

It was the kind of behaviour that roused not only Hans' fiery temper but all his dogged obstinacy. One thing was certain; the effects of this unfavourable meeting must not be allowed to spread. By the time he reached home he had decided what to do.

The next day he set out to call, once more, on all the most important men in the town, telling them of his audience in Copenhagen, the King's personal interest in the matter and his own unshakeable determination to see it carried out.

So sincerely wholehearted was he, so eloquent, that a few were finally persuaded into promising definite support—only a few, but enough to revive hope once again.

Gradually, one by one, over the next few months others were won over.

PART THREE

The cold, wet Bergen winter wore away, followed by a cold wet spring. The Egede family had been over eighteen months in the town now. Where they lived during this time is not known but it is probable with Fru Egede's elder brother Niels Rasch or with other relatives who approved their plans.

But now their small savings began to run out. Hans had no

regular work and though he records that he asked for, and was given, permission to assist at services and to preach at various churches in the town, he adds dryly 'I never received payment of any kind!'

But, slowly, the tide was turning . . . By May he had succeeded in persuading 'eight of Bergen's wealthiest and most respected citizens' to agree to support his plans. In June the Town Council reported this progress to Copenhagen with a petition from Hans humbly asking to be granted some kind of salary as he had spent all his savings and was now without any means of support.

In July the signing of peace raised everyone's spirits and an early reply was expected, but the weeks went by and no answer was received.

Meanwhile in Bergen interest—even enthusiasm—in the proposed expedition was beginning to grow. After all they said one to another, their town had never been lacking in enterprise!

Many who had remained silent at the meeting in the Town Hall now declared themselves willing to contribute to it. In all 'forty-eight persons of all classes came forward with varying sums of money'.

By the end of December, tired of doubts and discussions in Copenhagen but pinning their faith on Government help, the Bergen Company was formed. Hans Egede was appointed its president, leader, and commander, and at last, early in the new year, the long awaited reply from Denmark was received.

All was well! Both King and Government were willing to support the expedition and assist with its cost.

After thirteen years, through the energy and perseverance of one man 'the hazardous enterprise' had become a fact; the goal in sight, the dream reality.

Preparations now began in earnest and the newly-formed company started to draw up its plans.

Three ships, it was agreed, should be sent up to Davis Strait early in May. One, a smallish vessel of about seventy tons, was bought outright by the Company. Well sheathed against the ice and appropriately renamed the *Haabet* or *Hope*, she was to carry Hans and his family, most of the stores, and all those who were to help found the settlement.

The other two ships were a hooker which was to be fully equipped for whaling, and a galliot named the *Anna Christine*.

The hooker was to be despatched ahead of the other two with instructions to proceed up the West Greenland coast as far as the whaling area in Disko Bay; on her return at the end of the season to sail close inshore keeping a look out for the *Hope* and bring home news of her.

The galliot was to sail with the *Hope* but on arrival be sent out at once to reconnoitre and to barter with the natives taking on board 'such goods as could be procured'. She was then to sail home, if possible in company with the hooker, while the *Hope* would winter in Greenland and return to Bergen the following spring.

Meanwhile Hans himself, without whose initiative and perseverance there would have been no Company and no expedition, was living as he wrote 'in painful uncertainty' not only in regard to his position in the church but for his very means of existence.

By mid-January, having still heard nothing, he wrote both to the King and the Missionary College asking to be legally appointed with a salary pointing out, once again, that he was totally without means having spent all his savings in furthering the expedition. Not, however, until the middle of March was his anxiety ended and a reply to his letter received.

The king had appointed him Missionary to Greenland with a salary of 300 Rigsdaler (about £60), and 200 Rigsdaler for his equipment.

In the meantime a meeting of the newly formed Company had being held, instructions drawn up and a council appointed. This was to consist of Hans Egede as President, the Trader, the Captain and mate of the *Hope*, and three of her crew. Things were beginning to move at last!

On April 30th at the request of the directors of the Company, the chief magistrates of Bergen went aboard the *Hope* which lay at anchor in the harbour. The crew was mustered, the articles read, and Hans and the officers and crew took their oaths of allegiance.

Both the Dutch captain and the mate were experienced seamen—the mate having already navigated Davis Strait—a fact of great importance in sailing seas made treacherous by ice even in summer, while the members of the crew were all from in and around Bergen or from North Norway.

In addition to the Egede family were those who were to help found the settlement and winter in Greenland, among them carpenters, coopers, joiners, masons and fishermen. There were also three women to help with the household work, an accountant and a surgeon—in all about forty-five people.

Considering the little space available in the two ships, and the small amount of money at their disposal, the Bergen Company had made a good job of equipping the expedition. There was everything necessary for building the house in which the settlers were to live; stores and provisions of all kinds; 'rye and wheat flour; barley malt and hops for brewing; butter, cheese, peas, dried-cod; hard and fine bread; and barrels with wine, brandy, and beer'. There were also 'guns and muskets, pistols, sabres and gun-powder' and 'such medical stores as were in use at that time.'

To 'tempt the savages' and for use in bartering, there were 'brass and tin kettles, tin plates, snuff-boxes, knives, scissors, thimbles and needles', and, on the advice of Von Bärenfels whose men had found them very popular among the women, pieces of gold and silver tinsel and coloured glass beads and balls. There were also some toys for children.

The Captain had orders to sail north or south of the Faroes and then directly for Davis Strait. On arrival at Latitude 64° 15' he was 'to anchor in a place indicated by Hans Egede and the Council'. Here the ship was to be unloaded and the building of the house begun.

In order to ward off possible attacks by 'savages' the ship itself was to be watched at all times, and, since the chief object of the expedition was 'the propagation of the pure and true doctrine of God' everyone on board had orders to treat the natives kindly.

The Captain was promised a share of any produce that might be obtained, but both he and the crew forbidden to carry on any private trade.

All was now ready and in order and on May 3rd the *Hope* and the *Anna Christine* were to sail.

Thankfully Fru Egede looked for the last time at her long list of things to be packed, and with some pride at a row of neatly corded wooden chests and bundles which held the family possessions, while the children who had been taken over the ship by Hans were so excited they could talk of nothing else.

They had all grown enormously during their stay in Bergen, Paul and Niels especially. Tall, blue-eyed, fair-skinned and fair-haired, they now looked typical young Nordlanders.

All the Egede children had blue eyes and fair hair like their parents, but only Kirsten's hair was the true Viking yellow. Though straight it grew prettily round her broad white forehead, and during the years in Bergen had become long enough to wear in two short but thick little plaits of which she was very proud, usually, though by no means always, bearing good-temperedly with her brothers when, like brothers all over the world, they pulled them to tease or annoy her.

Petronella had been blessed with curls but these, greatly to her disappointment, refused to grow long and sometimes she would look with envy at her sister's shining little plaits.

The great day drew nearer. The sun shone brilliantly and a gentle breeze blew from exactly the right quarter; perfect sailing conditions! And then, suddenly, everything was changed! The breeze dropped—the town's gilded weathercocks veered right round, and what was known as a contrary wind sprang up. On May 3rd it was blowing still harder. Putting to sea was out of the question and the *Hope* and the *Anna Christine* lay side by side in the harbour rocking mournfully and tugging at their anchors.

Day after day the wind continued to blow. Their belongings all packed, their goodbyes said, the travellers waited and waited, the more faint-hearted among them seeing in the delay an ill omen, a forerunner of misfortune to come.

Hans' impatient, impetuous spirit found this last delay particularly hard to bear. It was evident, he said wryly to himself, his patience was to be tried to the very last moment!

For nearly nine days the adverse wind continued. Not until May 12th, to the cheers and waving of the large crowds that lined the wharves did the *Hope* and the *Anna Christine* sail slowly out of Bergen harbour. 'The hazardous enterprise' had begun!

As if to make up for its behaviour, the weather now remained almost perfect. Every day there were blue skies and just the right amount of breeze. Fru Egede and the other women on board sat every day in the little, cramped deck-space knitting or sewing and enjoying the sun and rest.

After the Faroe Islands were passed the ships headed for Davis Strait and though the sun still shone it became noticeably colder. At the end of the fourth week the first of Greenland's icy mountains were sighted—the jagged landscape known as Statenhuk near Cape Farewell. 'A forbidding and rather horrible country' Hans described it in his diary.

But more forbidding—and alarming—was the dreaded drift-ice which now appeared in unexpectedly large amounts and through which the ships slowly and painfully made their way.

Each day this became more difficult and more hazardous; the floes larger—often quite large enough to crush two such little ships however strongly armoured against ice.

On midsummer day things became very dangerous. A sudden gale sprang up, causing the floes to lurch and grind against each other and against the ships. There were ominous sounds as some cracked and split and great jagged pieces broke away and grated against the wooden planking. The wind howled, whipping the sea to fury, and stinging hail swept the decks. The crew cursed and swore, and some of them shouted abuse at Hans whom they considered responsible for bringing them to these treacherous seas.

Seeing a lead in the ice, the Captain hurriedly conferred with him whether they should enter it. There was a good chance it might end in clear water but also the risk it might involve them in more and thicker ice which, if it did not crush the ships outright, might imprison them so that they would drift helplessly—possibly for hundreds of miles.

It was a difficult decision to make but every minute was increasing their present danger and it was decided to take the risk.

But the storm increased; very soon the ice closed in again, thicker than before.

They were now in grave danger and when the skipper of the galliot signalled that his ship was already damaged the Captain lost his head and 'calling down to the cabin bade Fru Egede prepare herself and her children for death'!

Shocked and frightened by the abrupt and brutal warning but reassured by Hans, an arm round each of her little girls, Fru Egede kept outwardly calm. Deep within herself she felt sure of ultimate safety; a sense of protection; a certainty that in some way God watched over them.

Her calmness and repeated assurances that all would be well kept panic from breaking out among the other passengers and Hans returned to the deck to help and try to calm the frightened, swearing crew.

The terrifying hours dragged by. The wind blew in great gusts, shrieking and screaming in the rigging, and between the gusts could be heard the crash and splintering of colliding floes; the shudder of the ship felt as they lunged against her side.

But towards midnight the gale began to die down and at dawn all the floes had miraculously drifted away. A calm, almost ice-free sea lay ahead.

Hot drinks were brewed for the cold and weary crew and it is recorded that later 'in the privacy of his cabin', Hans 'severely reprimanded the Captain who by losing his head had endangered the lives of everyone on board'.

The damage to the *Anna Christine* was mercifully found to be slight and altering course the two ships sailed northwards.

On July 2nd they met a Dutch ship whose Captain Hans persuaded to take back a letter to Bergen and also to exchange one of his men for a member of the *Hope*'s crew who wished to return home.

The Dutch sailor, a boatswain who had navigated the coast for some years, was said to be 'fairly familiar with the speech of the savages' which, if true, was a stroke of luck and something that might prove very helpful.

On the following day, about two miles offshore, Paul and Niels excitedly watching from the deck saw the first Greenlanders, three fur-clad men each in his kayak—the light native boats built only of drift-wood and seal-skin and propelled by a single paddle.

'When we first saw them', said Paul, writing his early impressions of the country many years later, 'we thought they were seals! For my father it was a heart-rending sight'. And Hans himself wrote at the time 'Their first appearance seemed to me very miserable'.

This was not because he was surprised at what they looked like, for he knew what to expect both from books and pictures and from descriptions given him by sailors, but rather from compassion for them as untaught pagan savages.

In the early hours of the following day, piloted by the Dutch sailor, apparently quite unconcerned that he was assisting to safety men about to set up in trade against his own nation, the two ships threaded their way among hundreds of skerries at the entrance to what was then called Baals river, and anchored at a small island.

They had arrived!

7
Strangers in a Strange Land

PART ONE

Arrived! As the men began to make fast the ship, Hans stood beside the rail gazing landwards. Whether he saw much was doubtful for his eyes were blurred with tears, but in his heart was a deep thankfulness. Presently Fru Egede joined him and they stood silent, hand in hand. There was no need for words; each knew what was in the heart of the other. To both it was not only a moment of thanksgiving but of holiness; of re-dedication, dedication to the land of which they had dreamed so long and come so far to serve.

Now Paul and Niels came rushing along the deck towards them followed by Kirsten, her little yellow plaits bobbing up and down; Petronella, who always found the steep stairs from the cabin difficult to climb, a little breathless, some way behind. Hans turned from the rail and, still silent, drew his wife gently to him and kissed her. Then calling to the children to stay with their mother, walked briskly to the bridge where the captain was waiting for him.

Although it was barely two o'clock in the morning it was almost full daylight for they were not far from the arctic circle where the midnight sun still shone.

Away on the mainland a broad flat plain stretched away to the horizon dominated by two great mountains 'Hjortetakken' meaning 'the antler' and 'Sadlen', 'the saddleback'. The sharp peak of the former, in clear weather visible eighty miles or more out to sea, had been a landmark for the greater part of the last two days. Sloping steeply on all sides its summit thickly covered in snow, it was not unlike the giant Vågekallen away in Lofoten— in fact the whole landscape was very like parts of North West Norway.

Except for a little light breeze that ruffled the reeds along the shore and the cheepings of wild fowl among them, there was deep, unbroken silence. Of the three kayaks seen earlier—or of

Map of Baals river probably by Paul Egede but signed with initials "H.E."

any other human being—there was no sign; no sign of any habitation; no sign of any animal.

Baals river, so-called on the old maps, was not really a river at all but an arm of the large fiord known today as Godthaab fiord, and it was some days before Hans and the Captain could decide the very important matter of the best place to unload the ship and build the house. At last an island was selected and named by Hans 'Haabets Ø' or 'Hope Island'.

Being one of the outer islands it was not the best and most sheltered place for a permanent home, but time was precious, the house must be built before the brief summer ended; it was also important for the *Anna Christine*, which had now sailed north on her trading expedition, to be able to locate them easily on her return.

The calm weather held. Except for the cries of gulls, the cheepings of birds, and the occasional 'plop' as a seal surfaced and as quickly dived again, the same strange silence reigned; but all the time, somewhere in the stillness—among the skerries and the small rocky islands, behind the little stunted trees on the mainland, one felt eyes were watching, ears listening.

Kirsten and Petronella, who had more than half expected to be met by a deputation of polar bears and musk-oxen, with perhaps an arctic fox or two, were bitterly disappointed!

At last the great day arrived when everyone was to be allowed to land, the unloading of stores and the building of the house begun.

Long before breakfast-time the Egede children stood leaning against the rail of the ship impatiently waiting for the gangway to be lowered, their eyes roaming over the rocky island that was to be their home. But, as Niels remarked, after all the fuss about the need to build the house quickly, none of the grown-ups seemed in any great hurry. Even breakfast to which they were now summoned was apparently to take place exactly as usual!

'And make a good one', Hans ordered them, noting a rapid scraping of plates and a rather reluctant shaking of heads at various dishes—the Norwegian breakfast is a plentiful and prolonged repast. 'Yes, *all*', he added impressively. 'You boys will be needed to give a hand with the unloading, and Kirsten and Petronella must help Mama'.

Paul and Niels looked pleased. For once it seemed they were to be treated as they felt they deserved—like men. Anyway there would be plenty of time for exploring....

Seal hunter. *(by Jette Bang)*

'Hunter and dogs, North Greenland'. *(by Jette Bang)*

Paul Egede's house at Christianshaab, today offices of the
Royal Greenland Trade. *(by Jette Bang)*

Altarpiece by Professor Axel
Revold in Harstad Church of
Hans Egede preaching in Green-
land.

Library, Continuation School,
Egedesminde. *(by Jette Bang)*

Kirsten and Petronella looked more doubtful. 'Helping Mama' was sometimes interesting and occasionally fun, but by no means always; and though each privately admitted to herself she would be terrified to meet either a polar bear or a musk-ox, it would be wonderful to be the first to *see* one!

At last the long meal was over, the gangway lowered, and all the ship-weary passengers streamed thankfully down it. Presently, after a word or two with Fru Egede and a brief reconnoitre of nearby rocks to make sure no savage or wild animal lurked behind them, Hans called Kirsten and Petronella to him. Provided they kept well within sight of their mother they might run about and amuse themselves.

The unloading began. The timber, tools, and other material for building the house were laid close to the site chosen for it, food and other stores nearby.

It was hot work. The sun blazed down, far hotter than many of the travellers had ever known it at home. Thankful to be on land once more everyone was in a good humour and worked with a will. This seemed a land of promise indeed!

'You wait you!' laughed the Dutch sailor who was helping too. 'You wait you till you see winter come!' But no one heeded. At that moment it seemed impossible to imagine the gently rippling blue sea still and frozen; the dark rocks sparkling and shimmering in the heat, white with snow.

Along the little beach and among the scrub and boulders just above it, Kirsten and Petronella played happily. At first Kirsten had stood quite still just looking, staring.

'Come on', called Petronella who had run ahead. 'Come *on*!' But Kirsten did not move; she was remembering something; remembering another little beach, a beach where the spiky, green and mauve shells of sea-urchins could sometimes be found, and a little cave in a seaweed covered rock, the dolls' house she had never forgotten. And to her surprise—for she was happy—tears suddenly smarted in her eyes.

'Come *on*!' called Petronella again and then as Kirsten still did not move, in faintly aggrieved tones, 'I'm going on—by my own self'.

'No, wait! I'm coming', cried Kirsten, knuckling the tears out of her eyes and running to join her.

'What were you doing?' asked Petronella. Too young to remember Lofoten she had often been told about the dolls' house but just now for some reason Kirsten felt she did not want to talk about it. She did not answer.

'You've been crying!' said Petronella accusingly.

'I haven't!' snapped Kirsten angrily. Just tears in one's eyes couldn't count as crying. Then suddenly, 'Look! Oh—look! *Flowers!*' And everything else forgotten they both raced to where she pointed.

All the morning the work of unloading the ship went on. Crates and boxes, wooden planking, bales and bundles of goods lay piled up in neat and orderly heaps.

The sun blazed down hotter and hotter. Towards two o'clock Hans and the Captain called a halt. It was time for a rest and food. Backs were thankfully straightened and leaving two sailors on guard, everyone went on board the ship again. When they returned an hour or so later the two sailors were full of excitement. A short time ago they said, a man's head in a furry sort of hat had peeped over the boulders and then two or three others, without hats and with straggly black hair. They had called in a friendly way but the heads had disappeared.

'They come back', said the Dutch sailor. 'Natives here very curious—always; they come back'. And he was right. Work had hardly started again before Paul and Niels, whose enthusiasm for working like men was waning fast and were now far more interested in keeping a look out for 'savages', cried 'Look! Look!' And from behind the boulders and bushes emerged several short dark figures.

66

They were dressed in sealskin coats with hoods trimmed with what looked like fox fur; tight sealskin trousers and high sealskin boots—very much as eskimo tribes dress to this day. Most of them had the hoods of their coats thrown back showing their long, greasy black hair. Their slanting slit-like eyes were very bright, their noses rather flat and their skin dark and oily-looking. They carried spears and some had a fish or two dangling from their wrists. They approached slowly and silently. Then one, apparently a leader, stepped forward and began to speak. Hans strained his ears to catch what was said—if any of it matched the words he had copied and learnt so carefully in Copenhagen—but to his great disappointment he could make nothing of it and turned to the Dutch sailor to interpret.

'He say' said the sailor slowly and wrinkling his brow and soon revealing he really knew very little of the language, 'He say they help you unload if you like; natives here about', he added, 'like to help, they quite harmless'.

Friendly, helpful, natives! Savages indeed! Hans went smiling to meet the leader, who smiled broadly back, beckoned to his friends and in seconds—or so it seemed—a dozen or more short, dark, fur-clad little figures were darting in and out among the tall fair-skinned settlers carrying boxes and bales to their appointed places.

So great was their zeal that the sweat fairly poured off their dark faces, but with wide grins they wiped it off with a seal-clad arm and redoubled their efforts. After an hour or so, however, they appeared to have had enough and picking up their spears and fish departed as suddenly and silently as they had come. But next day they were back again—this time with a present of fish, a fair-sized salmon and two big halibut.

The building of the house had begun now and this seemed to interest them greatly. There were more of them than on the previous day and among them some women. Were they women? Kirsten and Petronella watching with Fru Egede were not quite sure. True their long black hair was done up in a greasy-looking lump on the top of their heads, and one of them had a baby peeping out of the skin hood of her jacket but—they wore trousers!

The day of ladies in trousers, except in the East, was some 200 years ahead.

Kirsten and Petronella stood staring, a little shocked.

'They have forgotten their skirts Mama!' they whispered to

Fru Egede. But their mother told them not to stare and whisper. Very likely these ladies thought *they* looked odd *with* skirts— which was probably true, and certainly they could never have seen such yellow, yellow hair. The women stared back and whispered as much as they liked. Petronella remarked on this but Kirsten tossing her little plaits said 'Oh well, *they* are savages' and felt very superior.

'They are not savages', said Fru Egede reprovingly, 'and this is their country; you must be polite'. And Kirsten was silent; but she still felt superior.

The fine weather held; the Greenlanders came every day and proved very helpful carrying stores and sods of turf for the house. But what really pleased Hans most was their apparent interest in the short service he held every morning, listening, as he wrote in his diary, 'with curiosity and attention'. So impressed was he by their behaviour that he mentioned it in his report for the Missionary College. Here, in addition to the descendants of the old Norsemen he had come to seek were 'other sheep': a whole heathen race waiting, and with eagerness, or so it appeared, to be shepherded into the Christian fold. . . . If only he could speak their language; understand what they said! Almost unconsciously he prayed that a way might be found.

The fine weather continued; the building went ahead rapidly and the house was more than half-finished when the *Anna Christine* was sighted returning from her trading trip northwards. Tools were downed as she dropped anchor, and her Captain beseiged with questions as he came ashore. What had he seen? . . . done? What goods had he managed to secure to take home? What news of the whaler?

Alas, from the point of view of the Bergen Company his experiences had not been very satisfactory. It was late in the season; the Dutch had been there before him and apparently snapped up everything the natives had to offer; every barrel of blubber; every pelt and hide. All he had managed to acquire was half a barrel of seal-oil! He had seen nothing of the whaler. . . .

Hans was worried, both at the poor amount of merchandise and the lack of news of the whaler. Though for him the missionary work was by far the most important thing, the expedition was being paid for by the Government and the Bergen Company, who would expect something in return for their money. They were not going to be encouraged by this extremely meagre cargo and the possible loss of a ship. He could only console himself with the thought that time had been short and this was the first attempt. Next year they would do very much better. This, he impressed on the Captain, he must make clear to the Company when he reached Bergen. The Captain promised and very early next day letters and messages for those at home, including Hans' report on the expedition to date, were taken on board, and to rather sad farewells the *Anna Christine* sailed away.

Now a whole year must pass before they could have stores or letters or any news from home or from the outside world again. 'The hazardous enterprise' was well and truly under way!

Their help in unloading the ship no longer needed, Paul and Niels were now free to amuse themselves. Fascinated both by their skin clothing and their skill in spearing fish they had already made friends with some of the Greenland boys about their own ages. The boys, fascinated in their turn by these fair-skinned, fair-haired strangers, crowded round them wherever they went touching everything from buttons to boots, repeating continually some words which seemed to correspond to, 'What is that?' and pausing expectantly.

Smiling to himself Paul produced a small note book from his pocket and proceeded to draw various objects—a fish, a spear, a sealskin boot. The fur-clad figures pressed closer than ever, grinning and exclaiming delightedly. Pointing at the objects Paul looked questioningly at each boy in turn.

His audience seemed to understand, and though he had no means of knowing how to spell the answers, he wrote down, as exactly as he could, how they sounded to him, repeating each one several times over to make sure he had heard it correctly. Even Niels, who had little love of learning, found this a good game. He could not draw, but he managed to collect a few words on his own account—spear; fish; sea.

Well pleased with themselves they returned to the ship and proudly announced the results of their labours. Hans was delighted.

'This is famous!' he cried. 'If every day you could do this we should soon have a dictionary! For a change *you* shall be the teachers and *I* the taught!'

This idea greatly appealed to both boys but alas, there were drawbacks. The Greenlanders, fascinated by Paul's drawings, would press so closely round he could sometimes hardly manage to use his pencil; and oh, how they smelt!

'Ugh', said Niels, shuddering at the very recollection. 'Do you remember, Mama, how you used to complain about the smell of the sea-urchin shells I brought home in Lofoten? Well, compared with these boys *they* smelt like . . . like . . .' he hesitated for words. 'I know; like myrrh, aloes and cassia—in one of the psalms isn't that Papa?'

Hans nodded, pleased, and not a little surprised at Niels remembering it.

'Do you think the girls smell too?' asked Kirsten. Niels said he didn't know but added he thought probably worse because for one thing, although the boys' hair was long, and greasy, the girls' was longer still—so there was more of it to smell! At which Kirsten wrinkled up her nose and felt superior again.

On the last day of August the building of the house was finished and all was ready for occupation. It was long and narrow, built of stones and turf, lined on the inside with wood and with wooden floors. It had a loft, two chimneys, and there were fifteen windows. Running the whole length was a narrow passage ending in an entrance porch facing west. Up in the loft was a second entrance for use if the snow became very deep. There were only three rooms; one for the Egede family; another for the accountant and other members of the settlement party; the third for the crew who slept in hammocks slung in rows from the ceiling.

The house itself lay in a long valley sheltered by low mountains. Behind the mountains was a small lake from which a little stream flowed to the sea on that side of the island, while the windows of the house looked out towards the mouth of the fiord and the skerries where countless eider ducks had their homes. Heather and birch scrub covered the valley; there were many kinds of berries and the little lake looked a likely place for fish.

The day was a Sunday, and towards noon, when all was completed, wearing his black gown, wig and ruff, all of which seemed to arouse the Greenlanders' deepest interest, Hans held his usual Sunday service.

Watched by many dark attentive faces, he began by blessing and dedicating the house which was to be the only shelter in the

70

long cold months ahead, and for his first sermon in the new land took for his text words from the psalm appointed for the day. 'Praise the Lord all ye heathen, praise Him all ye nations'.

They had only just finished the house in time! The next day a cold wind blew and there was a sharp drop in temperature. Hans stood looking about him, thinking deeply. Now his real work, his missionary work, his search for the lost colonists must begin. He was disappointed no Greenlanders had attended his morning service today but the sea was very rough, probably, he told himself, too rough for their frail kayaks. Later in the day however, the wind dropped and several of them appeared. They stood for a moment or two as if conferring together; then silently, with grave, unsmiling faces, quite unlike their previous cheerful selves, they approached him and began a series of gestures. First they pointed to the house, then upwards at the sky, then towards the high snow-covered mountains on the mainland and, repeatedly, seawards. Finally, pulling the fur hoods of their coats closely about their faces, they threw their arms around their bodies, as men sometimes do to keep warm, and then pretended to shiver.

All this was repeated several times. At first Hans thought they were warning him of the approach of colder weather, as indeed they were, but it was soon apparent they were trying to convey something more. Their dark unsmiling faces looked almost sinister, and they kept pointing again and again towards the sea. The Dutch sailor was called to interpret.

'They say "go" ', he told Hans. 'They thought house you build was a ship! They not want you stay here. They angry; they say when cold come not food enough for all! They *very* angry', he added cheerfully.

'But tell them we have our own food, or most of it!' cried Hans. The Dutch sailor did his best, but though he seemed able to understand a little of the native speech he was obviously not very proficient in speaking it. At last he appeared to have succeeded in making himself understand for the Greenlanders' expressions became angrier still. They pointed again to the sea, to the sky, and to the mountains and presently, scowling fearfully and muttering among themselves, departed.

Hans was distressed and disturbed. Apart from any desire to convert them he had become quite fond of these dark, friendly, little men. Now it seemed they had become enemies. He wondered how well the Dutch sailor had interpreted. Soon even his meagre help would be gone, for the day the house was finished he had announced his intention of walking north to find a whaler that would take him back to Holland. Nothing anyone could say would persuade him to stay and early the next morning he set off.

Whether he ever found a ship they never knew but they never saw him again.

Where the Greenlanders lived Hans had no idea, but he was determined to find out. Above all, he must set to and learn their language. Perhaps if he could find and visit them in their homes this might be the best and quickest way.

PART TWO

Though a cold wind was still blowing the next day was fine, and taking some of the *Hope*'s crew, Hans rowed over to the mainland. Apart from looking for the Greenlanders and their homes it was of the utmost importance to find fish and fresh meat before the really cold weather set in, both for immediate use and for salting for the winter.

Since they had landed everyone had been so busy with the building of the house that there had been little time for anything else, and except for the occasional presents of fish from the Greenlanders they had lived on the stores brought from Norway; this could not continue. Hans thought there were probably small fish in the little lake on the island but the salmon and halibut must have come from further away. He also expected to find game : hares, reindeer and possibly musk-oxen.

Rowing across from the island the wind was strong enough to ruffle the sea into white-crested wavelets, but even so, looking over the side of the boat it was possible to see that the water teemed with fish. None of the sailors and not even Hans himself, used as he was to the rich fishing grounds of Lofoten, had ever seen so many; but he knew only too well that in a few weeks this larder at their back door would probably be frozen over, and no fishing possible.

On arrival at the mainland they found an inviting-looking fiord later christened by Hans 'Priest's fiord'. The mouth of it formed a wide bay, a sheltered, almost perfect natural harbour. Hans was particularly impressed with it. Here, he said to himself, was the place to move the settlement as soon as Hope island could be abandoned: the place to build a permanent home. And he stopped rowing and resting on his oars sat gazing across the water seeing in his mind's eye the settlement house just *there* . . . a wharf and warehouses away to the right, *there* . . .

One day, after many trials and tribulations he was to see that house built; the wharf and warehouses begun. Today the thriving little town of Godthaab—the capital of Greenland, stands near the site. The house where the settlers and the Egede family lived is still there, almost unchanged, the home of the Manager of the Royal Greenland Trading Company.

As Hans still sat gazing, the sailors stopped rowing too, grinned and nudged each other. An odd fellow this parson! Dreaming away one minute, the next as practical and tough as themselves. It was to be hoped he knew what he was about in this strange world to which he had brought them, as knowledgeable as about the one above of which he was always prattling . . .

Suddenly aware the boat was not moving Hans came out of his dream and with a short laugh bent to his oars again and they began to row slowly up the fiord itself.

Except for the cries and cheepings of birds the same deep silence reigned as on the island. There were no signs of any Greenlanders; no signs of any game. The sailors were surprised at the variety of sea-birds, but Hans did not think there were any he had not seen in Lofoten though he was astonished at the enormous quantities of eider-ducks. In places the fiord was black with them! He wrote down a list of the birds for his diary. Many kinds of ducks and gulls; cormorants, little auks, great northern divers and puffins among them. He also cast a sharp eye over the vegetation and here his knowledge of botany stood him in good stead. He recognised various plants, many of medicinal value, and noted with satisfaction the large quantities of scurvy-grass—in those days the only remedy against the disease from which it takes its name. There also seemed to be many varieties of berries, and further inland he could see small green valleys where cattle might graze and corn or root crops be sown.

They rowed on keeping a sharp look-out for game, but saw none, and presently came to a fair-sized river flowing into the fiord which looked as if it might well contain salmon. Not far from its mouth stood some curious dark-coloured tents. Taking three men with him and leaving the rest to guard the boat, Hans

73

made his way towards them. As he came nearer he saw they were made of seal and reindeer skins stretched over drift-wood. Across each entrance hung a curious-looking curtain made of strips of seal-gut sewn together. Outside, among heaps of stinking offal and fish heads a slit-eyed, fur-clad baby played with a half-grown dog.

The dog promptly started to howl (Greenland dogs do not bark), bringing a woman from one tent and two men armed with spears from another. They all looked distinctly hostile and the woman snatched up the baby and stood clutching it tightly as if Hans, by his very presence, might spirit it away, while the dog showed its teeth and its coat bristled alarmingly.

Hans and two of the sailors were unarmed; the third had a pistol. Telling him to hide it and all of them to remain where they were he went forward alone towards the tents holding out his hands to show that he carried no weapon. As he came nearer he smiled and then repeated some words of greeting he had learnt from the Dutch sailor. Whether the Greenlanders understood or not they remained stock-still, silent and glowering, while the dog, growling and bristling, sniffed round his ankles in a most menacing manner.

Now three more men appeared; it was difficult to be certain but Hans did not think any of them had been among those who had visited the island.

Still smiling he pointed down the fiord and then seawards to indicate where he had come from; and then taking some small gifts—a fish hook, a packet of needles, and a knife from his pocket, came nearer and laid them on the ground, finally holding out some brightly coloured beads to the woman.

The men stood staring at these treasures; slowly their expressions changed; their faces broke into smiles, then into broad grins. But the woman never hesitated. In a second she had grabbed the beads held out to her and disappeared into the tent emerging a moment or two later, still clutching the baby but beaming with joy and wearing the beads round her neck! Hans made her his very best bow.

By now the men had picked up the other gifts but they still clutched their spears tightly and pointed suspiciously towards the sailors standing some distance away. Hans called to them to come forward and to show they carried no arms. Satisfied, the Greenlanders put away their spears and chattering happily passed their

74

gifts from one to another, stroking and patting them as very small children often do with a new toy.

Hans listened intently to their talk, hoping against hope some of the words might bear some resemblance to old Norse or indeed any European language, but coming sadly to the conclusion Greenlandic was unlike any known tongue. For the present he must rely on the few words and phrases he knew, and on signs, and he pointed questioningly to the river and then to the heaps of salmon heads. The Greenlanders understood his meaning and first stretching out their arms to indicate a large fish—exactly as any proud angler might do today—they then displayed three newly-caught but very small salmon and pointing at the river kept shaking their heads to show that the season for these fish was over. Anxious to see if they had any game Hans made signs he would like to enter their tents. After some conferring the curtain of seal-gut leading to the largest was lifted, and he and two of the sailors invited inside.

The tent was so low it was impossible to stand upright. It was also very dark, the only light coming from the entrance, but they were able to make out a raised platform at one end covered with skins, which was evidently the sleeping place; a cooking-pot smoking faintly on some drift-wood embers; and some fur clothes hanging up to dry. But everything was eclipsed by the appalling, indescribable smell and it was very quickly obvious the inhabitants knew nothing whatever of sanitation, and cared less!

In addition to mounds of filth there were lumps of decaying meat, half-cured fish, and skins and offal of every kind. Before he had been three minutes inside the tent Hans was sure he was going to be sick. One of his companions, unable to survive as long, abruptly turned and rushed outside while the other stood holding his nose, clasping his stomach and breathing loudly through his mouth.

Hans thought he detected the remains of a hare hanging against the tent wall but what the lumps of meat had originally been he felt unequal to decide and after another minute he and his companion retreated outside and stood thankfully breathing in fresh air.

'I suppose you get used to it', one of the sailors remarked as shortly after they returned to the boat, having made signs to the Greenlanders they would come again and bring more presents.

Hans wondered. He was particularly sensitive to unpleasant

smells. If, he mused, these were summer residences, what must the winter ones be like crowded as they would be with men, women, and children and with fires and lamps burning seal blubber oil; and his spirit quailed at the thought of living in such quarters. Even so, and if the inhabitants would allow him, it was going to be the best—probably the only way—to learn their language.

The sailors rowed sulkily homeward. The beauty of the fiord and its surroundings had no charm for them, they were interested only in game and they had seen none; not so much as a hare. And muttering among themselves they expressed doubts as to whether any existed.

Hans sighed; he foresaw a difficult time in the long winter ahead when there would be little to occupy them and food might well be short. But his spirits revived when they reached the island. Waiting at the landing-stage were Fru Egede and the children; Kirsten and Petronella between them triumphantly holding up a big basket filled to the brim with berries while Paul and Niels each clutched a bucketful of still wriggling fish.

'You have done better than we have', said Hans after these trophies had been proudly displayed and they were walking back to the house. 'One at a time! One at a time!' as all four children began talking together. 'I can't hear a word you say if you all speak at once! Now, the girls first'.

Kirsten and Petronella gave a rapturous account of their berry picking. Never, never had they seen, or picked—or eaten, put in Fru Egede—so many! And there were more at the house. Four big baskets full—enough for everyone in the settlement!

'And you boys, where did you catch the fish?' But Paul and Niels were suddenly overcome with giggles.

'They have put their expedition into verse' explained Fru Egede smiling. 'Go on boys, tell your father!'

'It's only rubbish', said Paul. 'We made it up coming home. Stop laughing Niels and say it with me'. And together they chanted, stamping their feet as they walked to mark the rhythm,

> 'The *little* lake was full of *fish*—
> We *hoped*—and took our *rods*.
> The lake was *very* full of fish
> And we've caught enough of little *cods*
> To fill a biggish *dish*!'

76

'Though I'm not sure', said Paul, remembering Lofoten, 'if they *are* cod!'

Hans laughed and said they were not, but they were good fish and it was a fine poem; he was very hungry and a supper of berries and 'a biggish dish of little cods' was exactly what he fancied, adding, as Niels looked rather apprehensive, he was sure there would be plenty for everyone.

8

Ups and Downs

In the dark polar night only the faintest glow showed through the thickly-curtained windows of the settlement house. Then a door opened and a thin line of light spread over the hard frozen snow. Wrapped in a long black cloak lined with fox skins, an iron-tipped staff in his hand, Hans Egede came out of the porch at the end of the house.

He stood for a few minutes looking up at the myriads of stars, brilliant as diamonds in the velvety blue-blackness of the sky; but only for a few minutes. To stand longer in that searing cold meant the risk of frost-bite or the creeping drowsiness that can so often end in a sleep from which there is no waking. He began to walk as briskly as it was possible to do with safety on the slippery surface.

Cold as it was he was thankful to be away from the settlement for a time; not only from its close stuffy atmosphere, the everlasting smell of oil and cooking and drying clothes, but from the grumblings and quarrellings of the sailors and other settlers.

He wanted to be alone to think and to pray; to be alone with God.

He was filled with despondency. It was exactly five months today since they had landed. In a little over three weeks it would be Christmas Day. Five months, and how little—how very little— he seemed to have accomplished!

Up to two months ago things had appeared to be progressing well. The trip to the mainland in search of game and the meeting with the Greenlanders in their summer tents had led to several more visits. Game—hares and reindeer—had been found, not in large quantities but enough to eke out the winter larder; and some skins exchanged for household goods. True, the skins had been crawling with lice and Fru Egede had held up her hands in horror and flatly refused to allow them inside the house; neither had they been used for the purpose intended—the first fruits of barter for the Bergen Company. On the contrary, they had been appropriated by Fru Egede for her sons!

It was Paul and Niel's dearest wish that they should be dressed 'exactly' like the Greenland boys they met and with whom they were always, and almost immediately, on the friendliest terms. They were rapidly picking up the language and had learnt that in the spring at 'a place not far away' great quantities of seals came ashore in shallow water only to become stranded so that even boys could—and did—capture them. But, and it seemed a very important 'but', to succeed in this sport one must, they insisted, *look* like a seal! They already had seal-skin trousers, not very different from those of the Greenlanders, which they wore in the winter at home, but only rough woollen coats and small fur caps. They must, they insisted, have 'parkas' like the Greenland boys. These parkas, usually made of seal skin, were a cross between a coat and a jumper with a hood that could be thrown back or drawn tightly round the face according to the weather.

Hans had demurred at first—the skins were not really his property—but he was overruled by Fru Egede. Their sons, she pointed out, could not be prevented from playing with the Greenland boys; it was right, and indeed to everyone's advantage they should do so—how helpful they already were as interpreters! And, whether or not it was necessary to look like seals, they must be more warmly clad.

'You and I, my husband', she had reminded him, 'have the fur-lined cloaks given us by our friends in Bergen; the girls their goat-skin coats and hoods. Besides, if what the boys say of this seal catching is true, they could soon replace these paltry skins!'

She had her way. The fur was cleaned, the garments made. Except for their fair skin and blue eyes there was now no telling Paul and Niels from young Greenlanders.

'Like that', said Hans to himself, 'perhaps the lost colonists will look. . . .'

The lost colonists! There were times when he had almost forgotten them. There was always so much to see to, to do. Not until the spring would it be possible to begin the search for them. By then perhaps he could hope to know a little more about the language. His slow progress worried him greatly; no other tongue he had attempted to learn had he found so difficult. Greenlandic, so important, so vital, for his work seemed to be defeating him.

There were times when he was almost envious of the ease with which his young sons picked it up in their play with the Greenland boys. But now they were gradually losing their companions.

As autumn advanced and the days grew colder, fewer and fewer Greenlanders came to the island. That they were all moving to their winter houses both Paul and Niels were sure, but not a word, not a clue, could they get as to where these houses were. Soon, Hans was afraid, his friends in their summer tents by the salmon river would move too. It was essential to keep in touch with them and try to learn where these homes might be.

He particularly wanted Fru Egede to see the place where he wished one day to move the settlement, and it was also possible Paul and Niels might find out more from these men than from those who came to the island. But there was much to do and again and again the trip had to be postponed. The weather, too, had become uncertain; for days cold with a blustery wind, then fair as mid-June in Lofoten. At the very first opportunity he had packed the whole family into one of the *Hope*'s boats, two members of the settlement party called Ulf and Thor following in another.

The day promised well. The early morning mist had thinned quickly. The sun blazed down from a cloudless sky, hot as midsummer, and the sea was as calm as a lake. Paul and Niels had begged to do the rowing. Hans agreed, but warned them it was further than they thought. It was, though neither would admit it, and both boat and oars were heavier than they were used to. Before they were half-way over they both had badly blistered hands but they kept doggedly on, though by the time they arrived Niels felt his arms were almost ready to drop off! But he quickly recovered and was soon eagerly hunting along the tide-line with Paul and the two men for precious pieces of drift-wood and other treasures.

Fru Egede was as enchanted as Hans with the surroundings. Keeping a wary eye on the boats they sat down above the stony beach where a little grass grew among the boulders, in the shade of a small stunted tree, barely more than a bush, which Hans said was a juniper—the tree under which the prophet Elijah had sat—in so very different a countryside!

Here and there small poppies were still flowering, swaying and nodding in the faint breeze; white, yellow and flame-coloured. Kirsten and Petronella ran about picking them uttering ecstatic little cries of joy. The poppies were new flowers to them. They did not grow in Lofoten though Kirsten told Petronella she was sure she remembered seeing them somewhere—no, *not* Bergen; somewhere . . . she stood frowning, trying to remember . . . somewhere . . . somewhere near a big, big, church.

'Trondheim', said Fru Egede burying her face in the bunch they had brought to her. 'Trondheim market place—near the Cathedral'. How long, long ago it seemed. . . .

Presently, taking the oars himself this time, Ulf and Thor following behind, Hans had rowed slowly up the fiord. The dwarf willows on the banks had shed many of their leaves, and all the eider ducks had disappeared. Gone also were many of the birds he had noticed on his first trip; and when they rounded the bend that hid the salmon river, the dark tents on its banks were gone too!

It was a bad moment; a bitter disappointment to the children, and a bitter blow to Hans. He sat resting on his oars wondering what to do next, when a curious-looking boat came slowly towards them down the river.

It was a boat such as he had often read of or been told about—a 'umiak' or 'women's boat', a long flat-bottomed structure, designed to carry some thirty people or more, but very light and easy to row. It was made, with incredible skill and ingenuity, of seal and walrus hides stretched over a frame of drift-wood—the sole materials available—and propelled with paddles also fashioned from drift wood. A stone-age boat, still seen occasionally in East Greenland even today, rubbing shoulders, so to speak, with the latest in motor-boats and even seaplanes.

In the boat were two men; the woman who had snatched the beads—still wearing them; her baby, three dogs and what looked like the remains of the tents and their meagre contents—cooking pots, skins, carcasses of game, dried and drying fish, tubs of berries, and barrels—filched from some Dutch trader—filled with seal blubber. Following behind was a solitary kayaker.

As they drew nearer the men and the women greeted Hans with friendly grins, while to the surprise of Paul and Niels, the figure in the kayak was seen to be a boy about their own age who had often come to the island and whose name they had learnt was Kusak. Niels could hardly take his eyes off him. To have a little boat like that—all to oneself! And so light and easy to manage. Unconsciously he rubbed his still stiff arms.

Soon the boats came out into the fiord itself. The umiak stopped alongside them but Kusak, observing the interested stares of these strange yellow-haired children, like most boys in similar circumstances was not averse to a little showing off.

He paddled here and there, every now and then shooting forward with almost incredible swiftness, then slowing down and skilfully turning. Suddenly he stopped, tightened the hood of his parka, and the next minute, with what looked like a mere flick of his paddle, had turned a complete somersault—kayak and all, grinning broadly as he righted himself and the water cascaded off him in streams.

'Papa!' cried Niels, breathless with excitement and clutching Hans' sleeve, 'Papa, do you think he would *lend* it to Paul and me—just to try? If *you* asked?' he added ingratiatingly.

Hans was busy trying hard to understand the talk of the Greenlanders in the boat.

'Be quiet and don't interrupt!' he said sharply. What *was* it they were trying to say? They kept pointing down the fiord to a big mountain, then to their various belongings and then to himself and the two men in the other boat. Was it that away behind the mountain they had their winter home? Paul, bidden to assist at interpreting, thought this was so; also that an invitation to visit them was being given. 'But only you and Ulf and Thor,' he added sadly.

It was too late today said Hans almost as sadly, and did his

82

best to make it clear that they would come soon—tomorrow if it was fine.

The conversation apparently at an end, Niels, rather more timidly, repeated his request.

'Most certainly *not*', said Hans firmly. 'It takes many months, nay, years, to learn to control a kayak!'

Niels had looked incredulous. A little, light boat like that! Given half a chance—and half an hour—he was sure he could manage it. . . . Not until a year or so later when he had had the first of many, many lessons, was he to realise that this was only too true!

'Tomorrow', Hans remembered, *was* fine, and as early as possible, with Ulf and Thor and two sailors he rowed over to the mainland. Leaving the sailors to guard the boat he and his companions walked some distance inland over swampy boggy land which presently gave place to a low but flattish plateau, finally arriving at the foot of a high mountain.

As they stood undecided which way to go next, one of the Greenlanders from the salmon river appeared and smilingly signed to them to follow him. After walking for a quarter of an hour or so they came to a wide plain covered with grass and scrub. Tucked away at the far side of the mountain, well-sheltered from both sea and plain by high ridges of rock, stood several mean looking hovels such as Hans had read about, crudely built of turf and stones, while away in the distance towered range upon range of mountains; steep-sided, jagged-topped, thick with snow.

As they approached, several of the inhabitants came out of the houses and stood crowded together, staring at them. Their faces on the whole were expressionless, but one standing apart, arms folded and scowling horribly, looked distinctly hostile.

He seemed to be a person of importance and held in much esteem by the others. Hung about him were many curious objects; charms carved from bone and ivory; claws and beaks of birds; while on his head the skin of some animal, the ears sticking up above his own, gave him a particularly forbidding appearance. Hans thought he was probably a so-called holy man or 'angokok', a mixture of priest and witch-doctor, and in this he was right.

There was a great deal of talking. It looked as if those from

83

the salmon river wished to invite the strangers into their homes while others kept casting sidelong glances at the angokok, standing silent and aloof, as if seeking his approval.

Hans began to grow impatient. Perhaps a little bribery was called for? Undoing a small bag he carried he drew out some presents : fishhooks, scissors, and needles, all of which were rapturously received, except by the angokok who coldly ignored them. Hans fumbled in the bag and took out all that was left—some brightly coloured beads and a tiny looking-glass, both intended for women. Out of the corner of his eye he saw the angokok glancing furtively towards these treasures, and stepping forward and making a low bow he offered them to him.

Still trying to appear aloof but trembling with eagerness, the angokok shot out his arm and seized them. The beads were instantly hung round his neck while at the sight of himself in the mirror his dour face broke into smiles.

A few chosen companions were allowed to have a peep at themselves and there was much chattering and laughter.

Hans seized the opportunity. He had long since discovered that the Greenlanders were very musical; the ones who came to the island had often held little parties, one beating a skin drum while others danced and sang. Now he decided to sing to them himself, and bidding his companions join in together they sang the twenty-third psalm.

It was evidently a success, for when they had finished the Greenlanders pressed round demanding to know what it was about.

'I told them', Hans wrote later in his diary, 'I had prayed to God that he would be good to them and give them food and nourishment'.

Though God meant nothing to the Greenlanders it was clear to them that good was being invoked on their behalf. These pale-faced light-haired people might bring luck. There was more chattering and the angokok, possibly scenting a rival, having consented with obvious reluctance, Hans and his friends were invited into the largest of the houses.

The way in was by a narrow passage about twenty to twenty-four feet in length and so low that it was only possible by bending double or crawling on all fours to pass down it. The house itself was not much higher, the roof propped up with poles of drift-wood. On one side was a window made of seal-gut, white and transparent, and on the other the sleeping place—a long low platform of turf and stones covered with skins.

Here each family had its own separate compartment, like stalls in a stable. In front of each stood a large lamp used for both cooking and heating, made of soapstone and filled with seal oil, the wicks of dried moss. Above it, suspended by thongs of walrus hide from a rack under the ceiling used for drying clothes, hung a kettle. This too was of soapstone, though some had been replaced by fine brass or copper ones given by the Dutch in exchange for hides and seal oil.

Although Hans knew something of what to expect and had warned his companions, even he was unprepared for the appalling stench and stifling heat that greeted them, for in addition to the complete lack of any sanitation, decaying offal, half-cured skins and half-dried clothes, was added the reek of burning blubber and of many unwashed bodies.

Seven or eight families, some forty to fifty men, women and children, lived in this house; all were not there, and more than half of the lamps Hans counted, unlit. What it must be like when they were, and all the inhabitants at home, he could hardly bear to imagine!

Once down the entrance tunnel Thor had been quickly overcome, but Ulf seemed unaffected. Hans himself, somehow mastering his desire to be sick or rush out for air, managed to remain inside for a while watched throughout with deep suspicion by the angokok. But after a time he, too, could stand no more and crawled thankfully out into the fresh air.

It was some time before Ulf emerged, apparently none the worse. He did not find it too bad he said. Due to an accident to his nose some years ago he had largely lost his sense of smell. It had some advantages but he had never expected it to come in so useful. But there, one never knew! And he added that he would not mind staying in the house for a time if Hans wished: he had the impression the Greenlanders would like it. It was safe enough, he was sure they were perfectly peacefully disposed, even the angokok. And if not—well—he whispered, he had his pistol.

Hans gripped his hand; he thought the suggestion a brave one, and something that could not fail to be helpful. Weather permitting they would come over in three days time and see how he was getting on. 'But,' he added firmly, 'what you are doing I, too, must do, even if I am sick day and night! Not yet, and only for one night, for I am needed at the settlement. Later, if all goes well I shall stay longer. It is the only way'.

Ulf was still in good spirits when visited three days later. He admitted he found the greasy, oily, and often raw food nauseating, but everything was interesting and he had learnt much, including many words. He was quite prepared to stay on a week if he could be spared. Hans gave his consent but it was nearer two weeks before they were able to fetch him home, for a thick fog descended, blanketing everything for miles around and lasting several days.

These fogs were becoming more frequent; it was colder too; autumn was almost over, winter setting in. As they rowed over to the mainland to fetch Ulf, Hans suddenly decided he would take his place that very night. Later it might be difficult, if not impossible, to go over and get back.

And so, greatly to Fru Egede's dismay, the boat had returned without him. She could only pray passionately that no fog might descend, no sudden storm arise. Next morning she was up early, gratefully thanking God for so fine and fair a day. Later, in the afternoon, she climbed a high rock and saw the boat returning. Hans was there but—she strained her eyes—surely there were four others with him and only three, Thor and two other sailors, had gone over? As they came nearer she saw it was a Greenlander—a boy; Kusak!

'Yet one more for you to cook and mend for!' said Hans, as he jumped out of the boat and kissed her. 'The boy has begged to come and his father has allowed it. He wishes to learn our language and to hear about our God. He will live with us and help in many ways, and I shall teach *him* and he will teach *me*!'

'It is the greatest encouragement I have had, my Gertrud', he went on as they walked up from the landing stage. 'A rich reward for the most terrible night I think I have ever spent. I—I cannot talk of it . . . What I need now, above all things', he added after a short silence, 'is a *bath*! So too does Kusak—the first he has ever had!'

And for some weeks, thought Hans sadly, as he climbed the slope of a very slippery hill, an encouragement it had remained.

Kusak had violently resented—and even more violently resisted—his bath, and looked suspiciously on all European food, but he had soon settled down, and was on the best of terms with everyone.

Hans learnt much from him and really began to make progress with his 'dictionary' as he called his list of words and phrases. He had been amazed at how quickly Kusak learnt. In less than three weeks this boy who had never held pen or pencil or seen a printed page, could write and read nearly all the letters in the Norwegian alphabet.

'He will soon outstrip my little Petronella', said Hans, hoping to shame his almost five-year-old daughter, whom he considered not only backward but lazy.

But Petronella did not care.

'*I* can *knit*!' she said in self-defence. 'Soon I will be able to make things to keep us warm. That is more use than letters here in Greenland!'

Hunting and fishing had gone well in this period too. Little snow had fallen and the frosts were not severe. There was only a thin film of ice on the lake and the *Hope*'s boats went back and forth to the mainland without difficulty. Fru Egede and the other women had as much as they could do salting, and preserving.

'Winter late but I think come quick now!' Kusak remarked, standing in the porch one morning and sniffing the air as an animal might do. And in less than twenty-four hours, heralded by a blizzard that raged all night, come it had!

After that snow fell almost daily. Searing frosts gripped the land; the lake was quickly frozen and patches of ice appeared in the sea.

All lay sheeted in whiteness. Except for the sound of voices and general clatter about the settlement there was a profound silence; not even the occasional flipping by of a gull or the now familiar 'plop' as a seal that had surfaced for air dived again. The fog swept in from the sea blotting out every landmark, creeping through every crevice and chilling one to the bone. All outdoor activities came abruptly to an end.

Penned in, day after day in their cramped and stuffy quarters, most of the settlers—the sailors particularly—grumbled incessantly. They cursed the cold, the short daylight, the monotonous food and above all, though each had come voluntarily, Hans Egede, who had brought them to this miserable and desolate country. Some fell ill; fights broke out daily.

Kusak too fell ill. He quickly recovered but was now obviously homesick and wished to leave. He sat sullen and unsmiling, refusing to speak, much less learn, and progress with the dictionary was at a standstill.

Sometimes for an hour it would stop snowing and the sun might break through, but the days were growing shorter and shorter; soon the sun would only rise for a few hours.

As Hans walked his dejection increased. Today had been particularly trying. After a brief fine spell it had snowed all night and well into the afternoon. A violent fight had broken out between two of the sailors. Called by the Captain to assist in separating them, Hans had been cursed to his face by one and threatened with a knife by the other. Calm had been finally restored but the question that worried him daily, nagged now like an aching tooth. How to employ these men when the sun would barely rise above the mountains and a grey twilight reign?

Nearly two months must be lived through before it would begin to grow really light again. . . .

He prayed as he walked, asking humbly but fervently for help, for guidance. . . . Suddenly a great beam of light shot across the sky; then another, and another. . . .

The Aurora! It was like meeting an old friend! Always, all his life, he had drawn strength and courage from it. As a boy in Harstad when things went wrong at home, and how often, how very often, in Lofoten!

He climbed as quickly as possible to the summit of the slippery hill. A great curtain of green and red swayed and quivered in the northern sky, parted, joined again, then suddenly vanished! It was only a brief display but the 'heavens had declared the glory of God'; as he walked back the crushing burden or responsibility seemed lighter.

As Hans entered the house all was strangely quiet. Fru Egede, Petronella in her lap, Kirsten on a small stool at her side, was reading aloud one of the most exciting of the Sagas.

Hans knew better than to interrupt! Going to speak to the accountant he saw the door into the crew's quarters was open. The accountant himself standing just inside. Usually this door was firmly shut and the noise behind it indescribable; now you could not hear a sound.

Except for a few men engrossed in a game of cards, everyone

was crowded round a long, narrow table where Paul, his fair head bent over a large drawing board, was covering sheet after sheet of paper while Niels stood beside him importantly holding a box of coloured chalks.

Whatever Paul was drawing it was being rapturously received. Oh's and Ah's of admiration and astonishment came from the onlookers. As for Kusak, he stood with clasped hands, all his sulkiness vanished; entranced.

'*You* try now!' said Paul, handing the board to the man nearest him. The sailor, a big, fat, good-natured fellow, took the pencil in stubby unaccustomed fingers. Breathing heavily with the unfamiliar effort, the tip of his tongue protruding as a child's so often does in similar circumstances, he drew something which appeared to call forth much mirth.

Another man had a try, then another, and another. Hans stood for a while, watching, thoughtful. No one noticed him and presently, leaving his business with the accountant for another time, he returned to his own quarters.

The bedtime story was over, Kirsten and Petronella both fast asleep in their corner of the room, Fru Egede busy knitting. As Hans sat down beside her she saw he was happy, even excited, very different from when he had gone out. He was not long in telling her the reason. Not only had Paul evidently found something of interest to occupy the men but he, Hans, realised how the boy's gift might be turned to even better account : a means of instruction for their heathen neighbours. For some time now, he went on, he had realised the difficulty there would be in presenting the very simplest outline of the Christian faith to men who, for example, had never seen sheep and lambs; an ear, much less a field of corn; a garden; a vine; even a loaf of bread !

And so it came about that between them, he and Paul embarked on a series of pictures, ready for the day when Hans would begin to tell the gospel story to the Greenlanders and, perhaps, to his own lost countrymen !

They began with single objects before going on to more complicated problems such as the Garden of Eden, various parables or miracles. Here Kusak was of the greatest help, not only in providing the names of the objects he knew, but after listening avidly to the story told him to the best of Hans' ability, the way in which it might best be understood by his own people. The Garden of Eden, for instance, must, he said, have many seals and whales—particularly whales—as well as musk-oxen and the other Greenland animals. There must also be many ice-bergs, and the sky and sea very blue—for good hunting.

Niels helped in this; his drawing was not very proficient but he was as he said 'quite good at icebergs', and he enjoyed filling in the blue skies and seas.

Meanwhile the sailors had taken to drawing like ducks to water. Most of them still preferred watching Paul, but a few began to try themselves while the big fat one developed quite a gift for portraiture and was much in demand drawing his friends.

Paul enjoyed his prestige as a teacher but was worried his paints and paper might give out before the supply ship from Norway came, and was rather grudging to Niels with the blue and green for the skies and icebergs!

Complaints, grumblings and fights still occurred; some twenty men cooped up in one room were not to be indefinitely engrossed with a boy's drawings or even their own, but for a time at least things seemed more peaceful; Christmas and the new year were not far off and then, little by little, the days would grow longer, spring nearer.

PART TWO

Christmas came and was a very happy day. Everyone, even the most troublesome of the sailors, 'tried to be good', as Petronella put it. To Hans' great satisfaction the short mid-morning service was attended by everyone in the settlement, even the most ardent atheists and free-thinkers lustily bawling the hymns.

No one had anticipated much in the way of festivities. There would certainly be no Yule log, as at home in Norway, timber was far too precious to burn; but certain unusual and appetising smells that had wafted from Fru Egede's cooking-stove during the last few days suggested that at least something extra in the way of rations might be expected. What was actually contrived astonished everyone!

Contrived was indeed the word! With five months or more before the supply ships from Norway would arrive it was imprudent to exceed the daily rations except by the very smallest amount, but within this meagre margin Fru Egede and her assistants had prepared what seemed almost a banquet, while as for the decorations. . . !

The meal was served in the Egede's own quarters, the scanty

furniture pushed back against the walls and two long narrow tables from the crew's quarters brought in. Attached to a shining red glass lantern which hung from the centre of the ceiling, chains of coloured paper, cardboard trolls and other strange creatures made by Paul and Niels, stretched from the four corners of the room. On the tables beneath were clean white cloths, and at intervals down either side small, coloured candles stuck in walnut shells shone gaily.

As well as the ordinary rations of bread, dried fish or salted meat, there were dishes of nuts, little berry-filled tarts, and great blocks of the dark, brown, sweet-tasting goat's cheese so beloved of all Norwegians. At the head of each table were bottles of wine and brandy and at each man's place stood a tankard of ale and a good-sized ration of rum.

In the centre of one table sat the wooden doll Petronella had received on her fifth birthday just over a month ago, a tray heaped high with gilded gingerbread balanced rather precariously on its outstretched wooden arms, and in the centre of the other, a huge cake smothered in cream, chopped nuts and raisins.

And somehow in addition to all this Fru Egede had managed a tiny present for everyone! Only a screw of tobacco, a pinch of snuff, or a couple of gilded nuts, but each had the recipient's name on a card with a tiny drawing by Paul and the words 'God Yule' (Happy Christmas).

Kirsten and Petronella wore their very best dresses. Long striped skirts half-hidden by snow white tucked and embroidered aprons, and red sleeveless bodices fastened with criss-cross lacings over equally snowy white blouses. Kirsten's little plaits, yellow and shining as the candle flames, were adorned with red ribbon bows, and red ribbon tied up the longest of Petronella's short curls. Fru Egede and the other women wore similar dresses, their best kerchiefs and head-dresses, silver belts and ornaments. Hans presided over one table, the Captain over the other. Toasts were drunk to King Frederik; to Norway and Denmark; to the Bergen Company, and to many friends and relatives at home. Later, when everyone had eaten as much as they could, tankards and glasses were filled again and there were more toasts. To the Captain—to Hans Egede—and his family—and especially Fru Egede! Even the roughest of the men had been touched by her thought for them. 'Fru Egede! God bless her!' rang round the room.

'God bless her!' echoed Hans lifting his glass and looking towards her.

Today in many strange and distant places men were celebrating Christ's birth but surely nowhere stranger than here in this small settlement house alone in a great white wilderness at the very end of the earth? And without his Gertrud, without her encouragement, her steadfast loyalty and her calm bravery, he doubted whether there would have been either settlers or settlement. . . .

For a short time after Christmas the weather was calm. The frost was no less severe but the fog held off and there was no snow. During the short daylight the men were able to enjoy some skiing and there was skating on the little lake.

Grateful as he was Hans feared it was only a respite. Born and brought up in a latitude only a little higher than that of Hope Island he expected the weather would follow much the same pattern as in Hinnöy and Lofoten, where short fine spells around Christmas were often a prelude to the worst of the weather. But though he knew the frost would be far harder and the snowfall much heavier, he was totally unprepared for the force and severity of the Greenland winds or the frequency and penetrating coldness of the fogs. He did not know—nor did anyone else at that time—that away behind the distant mountains, the whole country was covered with a gigantic blanket of ice, in places more than two miles deep, the home of the hundreds of glaciers that spill down at intervals over the narrow coastal strip.

Winds from this permanently frozen plateau were always bitterly cold, but now,

> '. . . winds thwarting winds,
> bewildered and forlorn . . .'

they were joined by north westerly gales roaring in over the frozen sea from the ice-bound wastes and islands of North America, or sweeping down from the very Pole itself. The same north westerly gales that had roared over Hinnöy at his christening but here in their homeland and in their unspent violence.

Heralded by a particularly fine display of the Aurora they set in. Like a pack of wolves, howling, snarling, wailing, they swept over the settlement. It was often impossible to hear oneself speak and there were many times when Hans feared for the safety of the house itself.

Fine, dry snow blew in through any crack it could find, and every day the drifts against the windows grew higher, shutting out the little light there was.

The cold was intense and at night it was difficult to sleep. The men grumbled and cursed and many fell ill. Fru Egede in additltion to her other duties was continually brewing hot drinks. The Egede children, wrapped in all the clothes they possessed, struggled valiantly with their lessons; even Kusak, used as he was to the climate, shivered as he helped Hans with the 'dictionary'.

For a day, half a day, the wind or the snow or both might stop, but almost before parties could be formed to clear the drifts and attempt to force open the porch door, the dank ice-fog came creeping in from the frozen sea; seeping through everything, chilling one to the very marrow.

And then, early one morning, the gales and the snow gradually died down; there was no fog; the eastern sky flushed pink and presently the sun, a thin, red-gold crescent, appeared above the mountains!

After that spring came with amazing rapidity. Everything dripped, the first sea-birds flipped by, and every now and then from far away came the crack and boom of a glacier 'calving' or breaking off at its mouth giving birth to giant ice-bergs that would presently join with others and in their thousands drift southwards down the coast far out into the north Atlantic.

On 2nd of March the first Greenlanders appeared at the island, among them Kusak's father. Seals, he said, were already arriving further up the coast and becoming stranded as he had told Paul and Niels they would. Spring had come early he added, the winter been a good one. A statement that caused some lifting of eyebrows among the settlers, and a shudder at the thought of what a bad one would be like !

He went off, Kusak with him, promising to return soon and take Paul and Niels to the seal catching.

Neither Paul or Niels enjoyed the expedition as much as they expected. It was not that seals were particularly endearing to them; they had been born and brought up in a fishing community where seals are seldom popular, and at a time when concern for the slaughter of wild animals was very much less than it is today. But they were kind-hearted boys, and the wholesale way the Greenlanders went about the business until they seemed almost drunk with killing and excitement and gorging on the fresh seal meat, disgusted them.

But as two members of the settlement who had gone with them pointed out, at least the Greenlanders had a swift way of dealing out death and probably the seals did not suffer much, certainly far less than if mauled by a bear or torn by the sharp teeth of a shark. And, as Paul remarked as he handed several skins to Hans on their return home, the seals *were* all the Greenlanders had to supply almost everything they needed—and not so much as a whisker did they waste !

Niels, not often subdued, said he felt sick. Apparently the Greenlanders had insisted on his eating some of the raw meat and he never wanted to eat it again, raw *or* cooked !

Hans was glad to have the skins. They were good ones and his cargo for the *Hope*, due to sail early in May, was depressingly meagre : one hundred and sixty fox and seal skins; twenty-five barrels of blubber; and a few pieces of whalebone—then much prized for women's hooped dresses.

In his report to the Bergen Company he declared himself 'greatly disappointed' with such poor trading results, but pointed out they had arrived too late in the year to travel far and the best goods had already been snapped up by the Dutch; and he asked, among other things, for a stout yacht to be sent out; with this he could make trips to the various trading stations early in the year and so forestall them. He reported all well at the settlement; his progress with the language; and the encouraging interest of the natives in the Christian faith. The search for the lost colonists would begin in August when the weather would be most favourable. He also mentioned the site to which he would like to move the settlement, and above all his complete confidence in the future.

It was a sad day for the settlement when the *Hope* sailed, almost the only cheerful faces those of her crew, most of whom could hardly get aboard quickly enough !

Up to the very last moment letters and messages were being written to friends and relatives at home. Even Petronella had by now learnt enough to print 'Love from Petronella' to her uncle Niels in Bergen.

Everyone turned out to bid farewell to the ship, watching and waving until she sailed by the last of the skerries and was hidden by a high headland.

9

To Seek and to Save

Soon after the departure of the *Hope*, Hans set out on the first of the many journeys he was to make; journeys by sea and by land. Journeys, as a Danish historian writes, 'watching for land-falls where no European ever trod; often blinded by the north wind whipping his face; often in secret alliance with the peace of nature or wrestling with its superior force'. . . .*

Journeys always fraught with danger, not only from the elements but the dangers of an almost unknown and uncharted country; the possibility of hostile natives, even of hostile animals.

Thanks to Kusak and the long winter he had made good progress with the language. He was never to learn to speak it really well, but he knew enough now to understand most of what he heard, and to make himself more or less understood, and it was a conversation with an old Greenlander who had come with Kusak's father earlier in the year that decided him to make this particular journey.

'Up the fiord Amerilik by name' the old man had told him, were 'many large stones'. Old people, who had been told by those who were old when they were young, who in their turn had been told it by their old people, believed they had once been the homes of white men. If Hans wished he would take him to see them.

It was a chance not to be missed; not only to see something of the country in the charge of a competent guide, but perhaps to learn something, if only the ways of these lost fellow country-men.

Hans was all impatience to set off there and then but the old Greenlander shook his head and refused to be hurried and later Hans was glad they had waited for every day now Greenlanders began to arrive on the island.

Apparently it was a sort of half-way house on the way to their

* Louis Bobé 'Hans Egede'.

96

spring and summer fishing and hunting grounds; but they also came out of curiosity to see the white strangers, especially Hans himself, 'the white angokok' as Kusak had christened him, who told of a great and mighty spirit—one who had all the earth and sea and sky in his power and keeping! They wished to know more of this, they said.

Delighted, Hans promised he would visit them when they were settled in their summer camps. Shortly after 'in storm and snow' he and his guide set off.

The Amerilik fiord was about two hours sailing time southward from the settlement past many small rocky islands already beginning to show patches of green through the melting snow. The fiord itself was wide—two miles or so across, running almost straight between steep mountain sides—an immense ravine, gloomy and sunless even on the brightest day.

After five or six miles it divided into two arms, one running north, one east. Along the northern arm was a wide but sheltered plain. The little snow left was rapidly melting, revealing grass already thick and green, and on the banks of small shining rivers dwarf birches and willows were bursting into leaf. It was very like Hans' old home in Hinnöy and he felt strangely drawn to it.

Here the Greenlanders lived for weeks at a time, either in tents or beneath their umiaks—women's boats—which they turned on their sides, supported with a few poles, and used as shelters. Here seal and salmon, cod and flounders were all to be found in large quantities, and here was—and still is—the best herring fishing in Greenland. In those days there were also large herds of reindeer, and many wild geese on a small fresh water lake a little way inland.

In spite of 'cold and tribulations', Hans wrote in his diary—though he does not say what the tribulations were—the two men penetrated as far as the head of the fiord and here, as the Greenlander had said, were 'many large stones'.

There was no doubt they were the ruins of houses—and the houses of white men for, here and there, if you looked very carefully, were patches of soil that still showed traces of having been cultivated; and no eskimo or Greenlander tilled or sowed. They were Norse ruins; homes of the old settlers!

Hans walked among them tremendously excited yet sad at heart. What fate could have overtaken these countrymen of his in this rich and fertile and seemingly peaceful countryside? He would have liked to stay longer but he was uneasy at leaving the settlement too long so early in the year. The weather too was bad; wet, bitterly cold at night with only a blanket for covering, and the small ship's boat for a bed; there was also the danger of fog suddenly descending. At the end of three days they sailed home.

Throughout the early spring the Greenlanders were busy sealing and herring-fishing among the islands and entrances to the fiords; later they moved further inland for reindeer hunting and fishing for caplin, a kind of smelt used for bait. In August there was berry-picking and the fishing of halibut and salmon began.

Used as he was to rich fisheries Hans never ceased to marvel at the wealth of the Greenland seas and rivers, especially the salmon rivers where the catches were often so heavy the fish was dried for use in winter.

'In their way', he wrote, 'the Greenlanders lived splendidly and joyously'.

Towards midsummer he made his promised journey sailing up the sombre Amerilik fiord to the camping ground. Except for the clouds of gnats, unheeded by the Greenlanders, but by which he was apparently greatly troubled—'in calm weather one cannot protect oneself against them'—the visit was sheer delight.

The brief Greenland spring was now at its height; the broad plain bathed in sunshine; the rivers sparkling; the grass nearly knee high. Birds chirped and sang and everywhere there were flowers. Great patches of poppies, white, yellow and flame-coloured, and pale yellow trollius as fine, it not finer, than at home in Hinnöy.

From under the up-turned umiaks, small naked children crawled out and stood gazing at him, their brown bodies gleaming in the sun like little bronze statues.

When Hans Egede came to Greenland most of the inhabitants he met were very much the same quiet, shy people still to be found there today in remote places where there are only a few Europeans among the population.

Up to the time of his arrival descriptions of them by explorers and seafarers had been concerned only with their outward appearance, their homes and their hunting. Hans was the first European to try to find out what they thought, their idea of the

world, their beliefs, their way of life together; a hard task for a man no longer very young and faced with one of the most difficult languages in the world!

Though in many ways their life appeared simple, in reality this was not so; it was governed by 'an infinite number of the most detailed rules'.

This applied particularly to hunting and fishing. Among other things it was every man's duty to catch as much as possible, and his catch was common property.

'What is greatly to be admired', wrote Hans, 'is that they have most things in common. They never let anyone starve and so put us Christians to shame.' And he goes on to praise the wonderful way in which they had adapted themselves to the difficult conditions and very limited resources of their country; their dwellings, their clothing, their household utensils; their simple but extremely efficient arms and implements; above all their boats, both the kayak and the umiack which he describes as 'unsurpassed from the point of view of inventive power'.

There was no doubt the Greenlanders were a brave, intelligent and resourceful people. They made the best of things and on the whole seemed happy.

All too often, however, as Hans was quick to discover, they were beset by fears. Some of these were very natural, such as fear for life and limb; of cold or starvation in their daily struggle for existence. But they had other fears which came from their ignorance and superstition; belief in powerful spirits who could harm them in life and destroy them in death.

These spirits were divided into two kinds. Those who assisted the angokoks or 'soothsayers', as Hans contemptuously called them, dealing out advice, punishment and revenge; and what might be called nature spirits, among them deities of the sea, the moon and the air.

There was Tornasuk, so frequently invoked that Hans was misled into supposing him the chief spirit of all. There was Tornasuk's grandmother, 'a large powerful woman who lived at the bottom of the ocean, from where she governed all sea-animals'; the spirit of the moon, Aningat, brother of the sun, Malina— 'whom he ever pursues across the sky'—and many more.

In addition to the spirits were other supernatural beings. Troll-like creatures who lived underground. They were said to have 'dogs' snouts and to be always laughing'.

Only through the angokoks and what Hans called 'their devilish jugglery' could any of the spirits be approached or consulted, and it was through these men, 'the lying, cheating angokoks' as he so often describes them, that hostility, even a plot to murder him, was to come.

But now no angokoks were present, only happy simple people ready to welcome him.

He began by singing as he had when he visited their winter houses, and when asked what his words meant he replied as he had done then, that he 'prayed to God to give them food and nourishment'. Having gained their attention by speaking of things so important to them, he went on to try to give them some idea of God : He who had created all things and was all-powerful. To make this clearer he produced a small globe, showed them where their country lay, and spoke to them of other lands and races. He explained a little about the sun, the moon and the stars, stressing that these, like everything on earth, were all in the power of this one God and of no other.

Next he spoke of Heaven, pointing upwards at the great blue sky, and trying to describe it in the way most likely to appeal to them.

'Up there in Heaven there is much that is beautiful; there we do not feel cold or starve; there we do not get tired and old;

there we do not die; there we will always be gay and happy, nay, shine like the sun', while Hell was described, as was usual in the eighteenth century, as a place of torments and every imaginable horror.

Such teaching could hardly fail to have an effect on the credulous, imaginative Greenlanders. Probably too the very simplicity and sincerity with which Hans spoke, and his repeated insistence 'I have not come only to buy blubber and skins from you but to instruct you about the Kingdom of Heaven' impressed them. They listened with the utmost attention and when he had finished crowded round him asking questions and saying, like the Athenians of old to St. Paul, 'we will hear thee again of this matter'.

So far things had gone well, thought Hans that night as he lay wrapped in a blanket in his little boat gazing up at the cloudless sky where the stars seemed somehow nearer than at home.

It would be more difficult when he tried to give details of the bible story; he remembered the trouble he had had trying to do so in his halting Greenlandic with Kusak. He spoke more fluently now, but there were things for which there were no Greenlandic words and he could only hope some of Paul's drawings which he had brought with him would help; and with a prayer for faith and courage he fell asleep.

The drawings, crude as they were—perhaps because of it— were an instantaneous success. Even the very smallest children wanted to see the Garden of Eden; the seals and musk-oxen and Niels' ice-bergs! Pictures of a lamb, a loaf of bread and a bunch of grapes produced broad smiles and sounds of wonder, but from the drawing of a cross when Hans had described its cruel purpose they turned away shocked. Murder, certainly torture, was almost unknown among them, they told him; but when he asked was it not true that in periods of intense cold, if food was scarce, they sometimes turned the old and feeble among them out of doors to die, they looked sullen. That, they said, was different. 'Too many people, too little food—all die. Little food, few people—all live.'

Hans wisely did not argue the matter at this point. For the present it was enough to have caught their interest; to have made known the existence of God; His power over all 'spirits'; His love for men and women everywhere; the freedom from fear for those who gave love and trust in return; and to have given some idea of the joys of Heaven, the horrors of Hell.

The fine weather held. Hans took part in several hunting and fishing expeditions, but at some time each day the tall, light-haired figure in the worn black gown could be seen going from umiak to umiak talking and singing and doing his best to answer questions. He was very happy and loathe to leave, but the ships from Norway might arrive any time in the next few weeks and he must be at the settlement to welcome them. He told the Greenlanders he would come again if he could, and if not, to sing and talk to them when they came to Hope Island on their way north in the autumn.

He returned home laden with gifts of fish and game, and before he left picked a big bunch of trollius for Fru Egede and his little girls.

The excitement when the ships arrived! They had been expected for a week or more now and there was keen competition among the settlers and especially between the Egede children to be the first to catch sight of a sail.

Every day when their lessons were over, Paul and Niels, and Kirsten—sometimes even Petronella, sometimes all four—rushed off to what they called the look-out rock, the highest point near their home. But the occupation began to grow rather tedious as day after day went by and nothing appeared.

It was Kirsten who finally brought the news. It was a particularly hot day. The boys had gone to fish in the lake taking Petronella with them, for though they complained that she walked so slowly, and talked so much she frightened away the fish, they found her very useful collecting and handing out bait and in other small matters; she also obeyed them more readily than Kirsten.

Kirsten detested fishing. The messy bait, the wriggling fish, the smell of the whole proceeding. No one, said Fru Egede laughing, would ever believe she had been born and lived almost four years surrounded by cod-racks!

In the heat the walk to the look-out rock seemed longer, the climb up it steeper. By the time she reached the top Kirsten's legs were aching. Once there it was even hotter. The glitter of the sun on the sea was so dazzling it hurt her eyes if she looked too long at it.

The skerries lay baking in the heat, their scanty grass already withered and dry. Hundreds of eider ducks followed by fluffy, newly-hatched broods swam proudly up and down. Kirsten, her

102

eyes screwed up, sat watching them as she had done so many times from her little cave in Lofoten. How much nicer a place that was! Would she ever go back there she wondered. . .? Suddenly two big white butterflies fluttered past and out over the sea. Following their flight she saw something mistily white, rising and dipping near the horizon. Confused with the strong light, for a brief moment she thought it was another butterfly then realised it was a ship—two ships—for just appearing over the horizon was another!

In an instant Kirsten was on her feet and scrambling hurriedly down the rock. In her haste she slipped, cut her knee, got up, then slipped again grazing the other and cutting her hand. Tears stung her eyes but she stumbled on, reached the bottom and ran limping over the rough ground towards the settlement calling 'The ships! The ships!'

Everyone came rushing and tumbling out of the house nearly knocking her over as they raced towards the headland. Her cuts and bruises were hurting badly now; big tears trickled down her nose. She brushed them angrily away leaving a trail of blood from her cut hand. To be crying with the ships coming!

'Go quickly to Mama', cried Hans, running with the others but stopping for a moment on seeing she was hurt. 'Plenty of time yet!'

But was there! Kirsten stumbled frantically into the house. Five minutes later, washed, bandaged and holding Fru Egede's hand she limped to the foot of the rock where Hans came down and carried her up. She sat perched on his shoulder, all her hurts forgotten as the ships sailed slowly nearer and nearer and cheer after cheer broke from those on board.

Paul and Niels and Petronella arrived just before the first ship weighed anchor, the shouts and calls at the settlement having carried as far as the lake in the clear, noiseless air.

Petronella stood by herself, unsmiling and looking offended. It seemed Paul had picked her up and carried her under his arm 'like a parcel'.

'Well what else *could* he do!' said Niels defending him, 'we couldn't miss the ships!'

For the next few days it seemed as if people would never stop talking! Asking and answering questions, reading letters and messages from friends and relations at home. Hans' first words after greeting the two captains were about the *Anna Christine* and the missing whaler. With deep thankfulness he learnt both had returned safely, though the whaler had been badly damaged in a storm and for a long time was feared to be lost.

Apparently there had been great rejoicing in Bergen at the news brought by the *Anna Christine* of his own safe arrival and the successful building of the settlement house. Indeed, he was told, the news had 'created a stir everywhere in Europe', and had greatly helped to console the Bergen Company for the very poor trading results.

As well as the letters and messages, there were parcels and presents to open.

'Better than Christmas!' Niels remarked, lovingly running his finger up and down the polished handle of a new fishing rod. Kirsten and Petronella each had a doll. Though made of wood with painted hair and faces, like all dolls at that time, they were dressed in real silk, low-necked, short-sleeved dresses such as great ladies might wear at court or to a ball, and were certainly the grandest dolls either child had ever seen, much less possessed. Fru Egede was surprised there was not more excitement; Kirsten and Petronella looked almost worried.

Alas, it seemed the dolls were not clad for the rigours of the Greenland climate. Not until she had promised to provide fur capes and 'proper warm clothes' did her small daughters begin to look really happy with their new possessions!

As for Paul, he was almost overwhelmed with the bundles of pencils, and paper, boxes of chalks and paints he received over and above what he grandly called his 'official' purchases.

Fru Egede herself received presents of clothing, and Hans snuff and tobacco and other gifts. Many of the presents were from strangers, sent in admiration of the adventurous family. Perhaps what pleased Hans most was the sight of the strong sturdy boat for which he had asked. He could hardly wait for her to be launched! Now he would be able to venture much further afield; forestall the Dutch at the trading posts further north, and above all make his longed for journey south in search of the lost colonists as soon as the ships left for home.

Meanwhile there was a great deal to be done; the unloading of stores; the shipping of the improved but still all too meagre cargo; reports to the Bergen Company and the Missionary College, and the writing of letters and messages of all kinds.

Among other items of good news brought by the ships was a letter from the Missionary College saying that in the following spring they were sending out a young priest to assist him. Encouraged and happy Hans began writing a long letter of welcome and instructions to be given the young man before he sailed.

The captains of the two ships began to grow impatient. It was getting very near the latest date laid down for departure. They had no wish to be caught in the ice. One day—two days more—and they must sail.

Hans had been so busy he had not realised how late in the season it was, and immediately on his return from saying farewell to the ships, he sought out the old Greenlander who had taken him on his first trip to Amerilik fiord and promised to be his guide if he went south. To his great dismay the old man refused to go! It was too late in the year he insisted, to travel so far south *and* return in safety. Even the new boat, displayed with some pride, failed to impress him. He remained adamant.

Hans was bitterly disappointed. Every month, every day the search was delayed, he felt was a betrayal of the Voice whose command he had obeyed. He wondered if the old Greenlander was right or simply did not wish to go so far? With the new boat and two, perhaps three, men from the settlement it might be possible to go without a guide?

But here Fru Egede put her foot down, literally; she completely lost her temper. Had Hans *no* thought for others! Necessary risks he must take, and she was prepared for him to take them. Unnecessary and stupid risks, yes *stupid*—and she stamped her foot to emphasise the word—she was not! With so much and so many dependent on him how could he even consider such a thing!

Hans' own quick temper flared up. In those days wives were expected to be gentle and submissive and not question their husbands' decisions.

But his anger was short-lived. Gertrud was so different; were she not, he reflected, would they be here, quarrelling and shouting at each other nearly three thousand miles from home.

And how shocking that the parson and his wife should be quarrelling at all. It was well that everyone at the settlement was out, fishing or on the last of the berry-picking excursions.

Ashamed, he drew his wife to him and kissed her. Of course she was right! He was a fool—a fool even to have thought of such a thing!

'Not a fool Hans' she said, smiling at him, 'but very foolish! And have you forgotten the other sheep—so near—and waiting to be fed?'

Hans had not forgotten; but soon the Greenlanders would be going north to their winter homes. Except for brief meetings then and perhaps some visits to the few families on the nearby mainland where he had had his first experience of their home life, little, if any, real contact could be made before spring came again.

But Fru Egede's words were to prove almost prophetic! Unlike a year ago when scowling, distrustful, fur-clad figures had pointed menacingly skywards and out to sea, some of those who had pitched their summer tents on the island came to announce their intention of staying for the winter too. They were busy repairing some old stone and turf houses on the other side of the island. Later they were joined by some of the families Hans had visited in their summer camp. Instead of scowls there were smiles; trust instead of distrust.

The sheep were indeed 'near—and waiting to be fed'.

PART TWO

The long winter wore away and though it was no warmer than the last, it was certainly more peaceful without the noisy, quarrelling crew of the *Hope*. At times the settlers grumbled and bickered among themselves, and occasionally there were mild rebellions among the Egede children. However busy he was Hans always tried to find time for their lessons.

'You may be living in a savage land', he often told them, 'but you are not going to grow up savages'.

Now, quite suddenly, Paul decided he had had enough of Latin. For some time he had been cherishing the idea of becoming a naval officer. What use would Latin be to him?

'To be a naval officer you have to be educated', said Hans dryly, 'and an educated man is expected to have a good knowledge of Latin.'

'Then I don't want to be an educated man', said Niels, who hated the sight of the Latin grammar. 'I'd much rather be like

106

the Greenlanders and *do* things; paddle a kayak, catch seals and walrus. So can't I stop learning Latin too?'

'As long as I am here to teach you, you will both learn Latin', said Hans firmly, 'so fetch your books and stop talking nonsense', and he turned to Petronella rebellious and—as usual—in tears over her reading-book.

Her slowness in learning to read was a great trial to Hans. He was reminded of his lazy young brother Christian, but Petronella was far lazier, or stupider, or perhaps both?

'But the words are so long!' she wept, 'and I don't know what they *mean*'.

'You can always ask!' said Hans impatiently. 'Six years old and you can't read even short words correctly!'

Later, when the children had gone out to play Fru Egede came and sat down beside him. She had overheard the conversation as she busied herself with the cooking at the other end of the room.

'Petronella is only *just* six, Hans', she said gently. 'You are too impatient'.

'Impatient!' exclaimed Hans. 'Why, I've exercised more patience with Petronella than with all the others and my own young brothers when I taught them put together! The child is lazy, and I'm beginning to think stupid as well!'

'She may be lazy but she is certainly not stupid', said Fru Egede. 'Will you let me try my way with her for a little and see how she gets on?'

'I should be only too thankful!' said Hans, laughing, 'but your time—you have no more to spare than I have.'

'Petronella likes to be read *to*', replied Fru Egede. 'As you know, I always read to her and Kirsten before they go to bed.

Kirsten can read to herself quite well now. If Petronella finds there is no story unless she reads some of it I think she will very soon learn.'

Fru Egede had her way. Some weeks later, returning to the house one afternoon to fetch something he had forgotten, Hans was surprised to see his younger daughter sitting alone at a table the big Saga book open in front of her, her small forefinger moving slowly along the page, as she spelt the words aloud to herself. Before winter came again she could read almost as well as Kirsten.

Throughout the winter Hans worked hard at his own 'lessons' as Kirsten called his learning and speaking of Greenlandic. Having a few families actually living on Hope Island was a great help. Steeling himself against the heat and stench of their houses and the sickness it always caused him, he spent as much time as he could listening and talking to them, and before the worst of the winter set in, he went over to the mainland to see those in whose home he had spent a night last year.

On one occasion the angokok he had met was present, looking, if possible, even more surly than before. It was clear he resented the pale-faced stranger in the long black garment, and though the words he spoke were smooth enough, Hans was certain he was plotting some evil.

Spring came more quickly this year. By the end of February the icicles on the settlement house were already beginning to drip, the snow turning soft and moist, and very soon there were small pools of melt-water on the frozen surface of the lake.

On the last day of the month Hans proudly showed Fru Egede a small black notebook. In it were short statements in the form of question and answer about the Christian faith and *they were written in Greenlandic*!

'I fear it is sadly inadequate', he said humbly. 'I have yet to unravel the mysteries of Greenlandic grammar! But it is at least a beginning, and as time goes on I can revise and add to it.' He was trembling with excitement and looking at him Fru Egede was reminded of an October evening nearly fifteen long years ago.

She was almost as excited as he was! Throwing her arms about him she kissed him affectionately.

'If I were the Lord, Hans', she cried, 'I would call out of a cloud "Well done, thou good and faithful servant"!' But as soon as she had spoken she regretted it. There was silence and Hans looked almost shocked. Then he smiled.

'God's ways are not our ways my Gertrud', he said, kissing her in return. 'And I', she heard him murmur to himself as he picked up his fur-lined cloak and prepared to go out for his evening walk, 'how little do I know!—"but the fringes of His ways; how small a whisper do I hear of Him!"'

Before the second week in March, the arrival of snow-buntings proclaimed spring had really come and Hans set about plans for his first journey of the year.

In the autumn some Greenlanders trekking northwards to their winter homes had stopped to listen to his preaching and told him of a place 'about six days journey north, rich with cod and salmon'.

The fact that many Greenlanders were said to live round about and that Dutch whaling ships called there to trade made him think the district well worth exploring both from a missionary and a trading point of view. But not until May, he was warned, would it be safe to go so far north, and in the meantime he was preparing for another expedition.

Listening to the Greenlanders talking he had sometimes heard the word 'kavdlunait' spoken. This, he knew, was their name for the white men whose ruined homes the old guide had taken him to see last year, but whenever he questioned them about these people there seemed always a strange reluctance to give any information. Voices would falter and a look of fear or guilt appear on their faces.

It was some time before Hans guessed the reason for this, and in the meantime he thought it wise not to appear too inquisitive. One day, however, the old guide spoke of some ruins, apparently quite near, among them 'a great stone house' almost as large as those to be found in the south where Hans had wanted him to go in the autumn. No Greenlander had built it, and most certainly not the Dutch, who came in the big whaling ships and who, he added, contemptuously, never built anything but little trading booths!

Though the Greenlanders traded freely with them and said frankly that the goods they brought for barter were better than those he offered them, Hans noticed they all seemed to have a low opinion of the Dutch.

'They do not speak to us as you do', said one man, using a word meaning roughly 'preacher' or 'one who speaks', and a name by which Hans was beginning to be known among them. 'They speak only and always of blubber. Blubber, blubber, blubber!'

Trying not to show too much eagerness, Hans managed to coax the guide and some of the older men and women to tell him more of the big stone building, and his heart beat high as he listened. From the description he thought it might well be a church, one of those plainly mentioned in the sagas and in whose existence, dismissed by many as legend, he had always so firmly believed.

To his surprise, for the terms 'near' and 'far' meant little among the Greenlanders, he learnt it really was quite near, actually not far from the other ruins he had been taken to see.

And again trying not to seem too eager, he asked if it were possible to visit this place? The old people had looked at each other doubtfully but the guide quickly settled the question. It was perfectly possible; the snow was melting early and quickly this year; in a little while now they could go.

Early in April they set out, in the new boat this time. A wind like a knife was blowing and although the sun was shining brilliantly, every now and then it disappeared behind huge black clouds and showers of stinging hail swept over them.

The journey took less time than expected for the new boat was provided with stout sails and the biting wind was soon turned to good account. Even the old Greenlander who had previously regarded it with a mixture of scorn and distrust was impressed.

They sailed up a long and very beautiful fiord whose headwaters were separated by a narrow isthmus from those of the sombre Amerilik fiord. Here they secured the boat and made the rest of the journey on foot.

The willow scrub was almost in full leaf; emerald grass showed through the rapidly melting snow, and the big flat-topped boulders were cushioned deep in newly green moss. Dark patches showed among the green—myriads of tiny leaves and buds. Some of the buds were already opening—little jewel-bright flowers. In a few days they would be fully out, moss and leaves completely hidden under their brilliant pink or yellow petals.

At times Hans felt he might be walking along the road from

110

Harstad to his uncle's house at Trondenes, or the winding track that ran past his vicarage gate in Lofoten. If the old Norsemen had wished to be reminded of their homeland they had chosen well!

As they walked the wind dropped; the sun blazed down. Very soon they came to what Hans described in his diary as 'a fine plain of very beautiful aspect, with lovely grass slopes'. And there, only a short distance away stood 'a tumbled down building, eighteen feet long by twelve feet high'.

From its shape and the way the stones were laid he felt sure it could never have been a church, not even a farm or homestead; more likely a store-house of some kind. Modern discoveries have shown he was right; it was definitely a thirteenth century building, probably a two-storied warehouse.

But Hans was not to be disappointed of his church. Quite near were the remains of another building. Here the walls stood only to a height of about three feet, but the stones were 'placed one upon another in an orderly manner and well joined'.

Carefully he measured the length and breadth. 'Eighty-six feet long by seventy-two feet wide!' This, he was sure, had been a church! He was certain of it. In this pitiful ruin his countrymen had once worshipped God.

'It cannot be doubted', he wrote later, 'that this is the work of our old Norwegian Christians.'

A strange feeling of happiness mingled with his sadness; saga had spoken truly; faith been justified. And turning eastwards where the altar must once have stood, he knelt among the fallen stones and the cold wet juniper scrub in prayer for those who had once served and worshipped here.

Meanwhile the old Greenlander, surprised that Hans appeared less interested in the better preserved ruin, had wandered off in search of game. Hans explored further. He found traces of small dwellings and here and there, as near Amerilik fiord, faint signs that the land had once been cultivated.

It was of course early in the year but he saw no sign of any Greenlanders.

He remarked on this to his guide. There was a short silence; then: 'They do not come here', said the old man shortly and Hans forebore to question further.

Before leaving they rowed to the extreme end of the fiord so that Hans might have his first glimpse of the 'Inland Ice', the great

Ice Cap itself, spilling over here in the glacier Ivisartok. This he describes as looking like a long tall iceberg, which the Greenlanders said never thawed, even in summer, though occasionally large pieces broke away from it to float with other ice down the fiord to the sea.

Late the next evening, cold, tired, and very wet, having been battered by hail and soaked by drenching rain storms, they were home again.

Two days later Hans was busy planning his journey north.

'Not until May', he had been warned, was it safe to go so far north, but as usual he was all impatience to set off. Any time after mid-May the ships from home might arrive. This time they would be bringing the young man who was to be his assistant and he felt it would be less than kind not to be there to welcome him. By the first of May he was ready to start. It was an early spring, he pointed out to the old guide, who grudgingly agreed but refused to hurry himself, and it was nearer the end than the beginning of the week before they finally set out.

It was still cold but the wind, though sharp, had lost its knifelike quality. There was what Hans called 'a travelling sky'—great white islands of cloud billowing across a blue background, and the sun when it appeared from behind them was hot.

The 'six days' journey' proved correct, but Hans' impatience was calmed by the beauty all around him. On one side the land, more green now than white, with brilliant patches of flowers; on the other, the islands and skerries and stretches of open sea where ice-bergs great and small sailed slowly southwards, worn by the weather into fantastic shapes and glittering like jewels where the sun touched them—emerald, blue, silver. Seals lay basking on rocks and floes; sea-birds of all kinds flew overhead, and in places the sea was darkened by enormous shoals of fish.

Bays and harbours where the Dutch came to trade were pointed out, and at last they arrived at one of the most popular, Delfthaven, now known as Fiskefiorden, or Fishfiord.

The travelling Greenlanders had not exaggerated. Here indeed was a place that fulfilled all a trader's dreams! As Hans wrote later in his report to the Bergen Company there was hunting; a beautiful mere where fresh water fish were to be had both winter and summer; pasture for cattle, a known centre for trading with the

112

Danish Royal Family in Greenlandic dress. (1952)

Present day confirmation candidates in national dress. *(by Christian Vibe)*

Kayak and umiak. *(Woodcut by a Greenlander)*

Statue of Hans Egede by Nicolay Schiöll unveiled in Oslo in May 1965.

Church ruins at Kakortok. *(after a drawing made in 1830)*

Greenlanders; an excellent harbour. It was also possible to approach by land as well as by sea.

The Dutch, he reflected, knew well what they were about. But they had no real right there, Greenland was still a Danish colony, if a sadly neglected one. They were not going to take kindly to competition and he foresaw trouble with them.

Still further north, 'six to eight days' boat journey', said the Greenlander, was a place called Nepisat. Here the Dutch came after whales, though they also took the salmon and halibut which were there 'in great abundance'.

Next year, Hans told him he would travel to Nepisat and see it for himself but now he must return home; he was short of time; bad weather, especially fog, must be allowed for. He was fortunate; the fine weather continued. At mid-day on the eighteenth, Fru Egede, taking an anxious hour off from her cooking and climbing to the top of the look-out rock, presently saw the little boat approaching, her sails set and her sturdy prow rising and dipping in the choppy sea.

Five days later, towards evening, the two ships from Norway arrived and Hans joyfully greeted a tall, pale, grave-looking young man; his first assistant priest—Albert Top.

PART THREE

The coming of Albert Top was a great help to Hans once the task of instructing him in his work was over.

Having carefully studied all the information and language notes sent him the young man found things less strange than he might otherwise have done. During the long voyage he had worked hard at Greenlandic, and was so quick to learn that with a little practice Hans saw he would soon speak it as well, if not better, than himself.

Fru Egede was concerned that he looked so pale and thin, and took special care with his food, but he did not seem to tire when Hans took him on long and arduous walks, and was particularly skilful in handling a boat. On the whole a rather grave young man, he got on well with everyone at the settlement, and his quiet ways seemed to appeal to the Greenlanders. Sometimes his youthfulness—he was only twenty-six—asserted itself, his grave manner left him, and he enjoyed what today might be called 'ragging' with Paul and Niels.

Flattered by the attention from someone so much older, they hung on his words and fetched and carried for him like little dogs.

Hans was amused and pleased. He thought it good for his boys to have some male companionship other than his own and that of the much older settlers, or the gentle but ignorant Greenland boys; from Albert Top, he was sure, his sons would learn nothing but good. Like his own father he had wisely made no attempt to persuade them in their choice of a career, but a few years later when Paul made the hard decision to abandon his dream of becoming a naval officer and announced his intention to be a missionary like himself, he strongly suspected the influence, conscious or unconscious, of his young assistant.

With so reliable a young man Hans felt he would be able to leave the settlement for short periods less torn by the fears and misgivings which however hard he fought against them and accused himself of lack of faith, always beset him the moment it was out of his sight.

During his two visits there the previous year he had particularly noticed the lush grass and fertile-looking plains near the head of Amerilik fiord, and had made up his mind to sow grain and other seeds there. The time for doing this was overdue; the weather was gloriously fine, and he was loath to leave the matter longer. With the help of a couple of men from the settlement he need not be away more than a day. There would only be time to burn and rake away the old grass, no ploughing.

'A curious form of husbandry' as he dryly remarked to Albert Top when explaining the matter to him, 'but an experiment'. And he smiled to himself as he used the word in connection with crops. What memories it brought back! The small and precious strips of land among the boulders at home in Harstad. The hard-won permission to use one of them; his father's rather grudging congratulations on any successes; his anger and the gloom into which the whole household would be plunged at the far more frequent failures. But it had been worth it for the experience, and, he was confident, it would be worth it now.

From the days of Erik-the-Red corn had had to be sent from home and the failure of supply ships to arrive could spell starvation. If grain could be induced to ripen in the short Greenland summer one great hazard to life would have been removed. That it had been tried—and failed—he knew from the sagas, but there was no harm in trying again. And so, only a little more than a week after Albert Top's arrival, already his confidence in the young man was such that on the last day of the month Hans set out, leaving him in charge of the settlement.

About three weeks later Hans returned to see how his experiment was faring, and yielding to their entreaties took Fru Egede and his two little girls with him for a brief holiday.

They set out immediately after evensong one Sunday taking food and blankets and cooking pots with them, and spent the long light night and the whole of the next day near the head of the fiord.

Growth is always rapid in the brief northern spring but even Hans was surprised to see that the grain was 'already a finger's breadth above the soil', the other crops pushing up sturdy little leaf-blades. The experiment was going well!

In the late afternoon of the day after their arrival they were greeted by several Greenlanders, among them some women and children to whom Fru Egede and the two fair-haired little girls were evidently a great source of interest, some of the women shyly attempting to stroke the children's shining hair.

Hans pointed out two little girls of about the same age as his daughters and suggested to his wife that they should play together, but Fru Egede firmly refused to allow it, insisting that the little Greenlanders' heads were swarming with lice.

'*All* Greenlanders swarm with them', objected Hans, laughing.

'It is different for you and the boys', replied Fru Egede, 'you are taller. These children are the same height, and I am not sure', she added thoughtfully, 'that lice don't *jump*. Anyway, I say no!'

Hans looked disappointed but Kirsten and Petronella drew closer to their mother and Kirsten gave a little shiver.

Very soon many more Greenlanders appeared, among them some to whom Hans had sung and talked the year before. They crowded round begging him to do so again.

Telling them, as his Master before him had told another insistent crowd, to sit down upon the green grass, he presently sang a psalm followed by a hymn in which Fru Egede and the two children joined. Then telling the Greenlanders to kneel he pointed upward at the clear blue sky and repeated the Lord's Prayer, afterwards interpreting it for them to the best of his

115

ability and promising to sing and talk to them again on their journey northwards in the autumn.

Late the same evening Hans and his wife rowed home, the two little girls lying half-asleep in the bottom of the boat, the sea smooth and calm as a lake in summer. The sun had not long set and the sky was still light, streaked with the colours of its afterglow; it would not be long before it rose again for tomorrow would be mid-summer day.

'At home', murmured Fru Egede with one of the rare traces of home-sickness in her voice Hans had heard, 'it would still be shining!'

Very soon after this preparations began for the great journey south postponed from last year. Having failed to find any trace of the old settlers except what he rightly believed to be their homes, Hans had reluctantly come to the conclusion that many of the dark legends he had heard or read held more than a grain of truth, and the sad fact must be faced that in this part of Greenland anyway, no survivors of those he had come so far to seek survived.

Everything seemed to him to point to some terrible slaughter, probably by a wandering eskimo tribe that had swooped down on the fertile farmlands and happy homesteads and by sheer weight of numbers practically exterminated the inhabitants. Pride of race apart, he could not bring himself to believe that Norsemen armed with the bows and arrows of the time, or even with their bare fists, could not otherwise have been more than a match for primitive eskimos!

This slaughter might well have been at the hands of remote ancestors of those with whom he talked today; the dark tales he heard, memories handed on from generation to generation; the frequent looks of fear and guilt a lingering shame for them in the present peace-loving descendents.

Even so, he argued with himself, a few Norsemen might surely have survived, mingled with the invading tribe and eventually been absorbed into it? But although he kept a sharp look-out for such signs as might be expected in so mixed a race—noses not quite so flat; blue, less slit-like eyes; hair finer and lighter than the coarse black locks of his neighbours—he had so far seen none. This, however, did not rule out the possibility that men of

116

mixed descent might not be found further south, where it was generally agreed the colonists had first settled; the East and West Bygd of the sagas; and only in East Bygd, so confidently assumed to be on the ice-bound eastern coast, Hans believed men of pure Norse descent would be found—a belief he was to hold to his dying day—and his hopes ran high as preparations for the long journey went ahead, and the hour for which he had prayed and laboured so long drew nearer.

The Bergen Company had proposed this expedition should travel overland. To this Hans had written his disagreement in the strongest possible terms, pointing out the impossibility of climbing icy cliffs, crossing glaciers and deep snow, for men who in addition to guns would have to carry provisions for at least two weeks.

He had very little faith in the maps of the time, having frequently been misled by them, and he particularly distrusted the existence of two big straits shown as cutting through the narrowest part of the country. On the other hand he thought the East Bygd might be reached partly by sea and partly by way of another, smaller, strait, said to lead from the head of a fiord on the west coast to one on the east.

Privately he doubted the existence of this strait too. The east coast, he was convinced, would be reached by sea, but only by rounding Cape Farewell and somehow penetrating the barrier of ice that had defeated so many.

No answer could be received to this letter before he left but he felt fully justified in trusting to his own judgement and on August 9th with ten men one of whom, the mate Erik Larsen, left a detailed diary of the expedition, he set out — by sea.

On August 16th, in fine sunny weather, Hans and his men reached the mouth of Sermelik fiord, where drift ice from the sea mingled with glacier ice from the land. Successfully passing through this they turned eastwards and rowing up another, smaller, fiord, came upon a large camp—eighteen tents in all—and many Greenlanders who appeared friendly and pleased to see them.

Leading out of this fiord was a narrow sound and Hans steered towards the head of it in the hope of finding the small strait supposed to lead to the east coast.

On either side there were the ruins of stone houses, and camping near them he and his men spent the night.

117

The Greenlanders here appeared very lively and talkative. Listening carefully to them Hans noticed their pronunciation of certain words was different from that of the Greenlanders further north. He thought he detected a trace of old Norse, even Latin, in some of them, and he looked expectantly for signs of a mixed race but saw none.

The following day they rowed up several small fiords and inlets, camping for the night by a little sandy creek.

'A beautiful place', Hans wrote of it, 'with fine grass slopes, meadows and a good winter harbour' and where it was very plain the soil had once been cultivated.

Rowing up an arm of the same fiord the following day they saw the remains of many stone houses under the long, lush grass and—what was rare further north, a small birch wood. The trunks of the trees are described as being 'thick as a man's leg, but crooked' and 'not more than two fathoms high'—a nautical touch which sounds as if Hans was quoting from the mate's diary.

Sailing in and out of the fiords in the fine sunny weather, though very pleasant, had taken much precious time. No sign of the small strait had been seen, nor had any Greenlander they questioned ever heard of it. Hans now turned seawards and sailing close inshore steered south for two days, keeping a sharp look-out as they passed the place where the two big straits were so confidently marked on the map but seeing no sign of them.

Still heading South they sailed on for another two days and had come within a mile of Nanortalik when the weather suddenly broke. There were heavy rainstorms and squalls of cold blustery wind. The men were unwilling to go on. They were fearful the food would run short and any landfall they might make be dangerous, insisting that the Greenlanders of the south had a bad reputation; that they were wild and savage, some even said cannibals.

Except in regard to food Hans discounted these statements but he was well aware of the danger of continuing further south in bad weather. There was also the long journey back to consider; they were already well over five hundred miles from home, with the risk of bad storms and the ever-present but increasing danger of fog so late in the year.

Sadly, reluctantly, and with a very heavy heart, he gave the order to turn back.

During the next few days, almost as if in compensation for so tremendous a disappointment, he was to have some quite unlooked for happiness. Two unexpected things happened; the finding of Hvalsö church; and—what seemed hardly short of a miracle—the restoring of a man's sight.

During the stormy weather they had been blown slightly off course and now found themselves in one of the most beautiful parts of Greenland.

Late one evening, sailing past many flat green islands into Kakortok fiord and looking for a sheltered place to camp they came upon the ruins of Hvalsö church. These ruins, some of the most famous and best preserved of all Norse buildings, stand today almost exactly as Hans saw and described them on that summer evening of 1723.

'The church', he wrote, 'is twenty-eight feet long and a little more than twenty-five feet wide . . . the wall still standing to a height of twelve to fifteen feet and six feet thick, with two doors on the south side and a large one on the west. On the northern side one window only, but on the southern four, besides a large window in each gable'. The wall itself he describes as 'well preserved; the stones large, plain and smooth as if hewn; the whole building well planned and artistically designed, with a walled church yard'.

He also mentions the remains of a large house near the church 'the walls still standing above a man's height'.

Many Greenlanders were camped round about and they stood watching as Hans and his men walked about the church ruins, measuring and talking among themselves. The big house, volunteered one old man, had been built by Kavdlunait—white men—though it was said it had never really been a house, only a place where people met and talked; for what purpose no one knew. Hans and his friends were white men, perhaps they could tell?

Hans seized the opportunity. It had indeed been a house, he replied, no less than the house of God. He who ruled over all; who had made men and animals, the earth and sea and sky. Bad men, he went on, had destroyed the house, and as he spoke he noted the swift furtive glances from one man to another and the now familiar troubled or guilty look spread over many faces.

Very briefly, and in the way he thought they could best understand, he tried to explain the Christian faith to the small, atten-

119

tive fur-clad figures. It was to this Christian God and to His Son who had died to help them they must pray, he told them; not to spirits, for this was the God who ruled over all and from Him, and Him alone, came goodness, help, and healing.

He had hardly spoken the word 'healing' when a Greenlander pulled at his sleeve and pointed to a man, his arms outstretched being half-pulled, half-pushed by two other men, towards him.

The man appeared blind. His eyes were tightly shut, the lids glued down and crusted with horrible running sores. Healing—sight—was what he craved beyond anything. Here perhaps was someone who could help?

Hans knew little of medicine; only the rough and ready first-aid of his time. The word disinfectant had yet to be invented but it was known that wine and spirits, particularly brandy, often helped in the healing of wounds.

'Of myself', he told the Greenlander, 'I can do nothing; but I will pray for help to Him about whom I have been trying to tell you. But you too must believe in Him and pray to Him yourself, asking that through His Son who died for you, as for all men, you may be healed. Then, if it is His will for you, so it will be'. And telling his men to keep the other Greenlanders at a distance, he asked the blind man to kneel down.

While Hans had been talking the sky had darkened and now it looked as if a storm was blowing up. There was no time to lose. Ripping a piece off his shirt he tore it into small strips soaking them in brandy from a flask he always carried for emergencies on his journeys. Then after a brief prayer he began very gently to wipe away all he could of the mixture of dirt, dried blood, and matter from the man's sealed lids.

It must have been painful but the Greenlander made no sound even when Hans held pieces of the linen soaked in the fiery spirit for a little against each reddened, now almost raw, eyelid. Presently, throwing the linen away, he took the man by the hands telling him to stand up and open his eyes.

Stumbling to his feet the Greenlander obeyed, standing for a moment or two as if dazed.

Silently praying, Hans watched him. Slowly the sealed lids seemed to move; slowly to separate; to flutter; then suddenly almost to tear themselves apart. A moment later Greenlandic words meaning 'I see! I see!' echoed through the ruins, across the fiord, among the islands, away to the far off mountains;

120

echoed even above the sound of distant thunder and the deafening noise of the torrential rain that began to pour down as the storm that had been brewing, suddenly broke.

The storm had blown itself out and the men were rowing briskly looking for a sheltered place to spend the night. Hans had stopped for a moment and sat resting on his oars. His eyes were closed and his lips moved slightly. Was it a prayer of thanksgiving? His heart must have been filled with gratitude. Was he remembering something—words, half-forgotten until now, read long ago in his student days in Copenhagen? Words spoken by the great sixteenth century French surgeon Ambroise Paré, 'I treated him : God healed him'.

Thirteen years later Hans was to meet the once blind Greenlander again—his eyes now bright and healthy.

'I believe no longer in spirits', he told him, 'and so I do not pray to them; I pray now only to your Christian God and to His Son.'

On September 14th, a little over five weeks since they had left it, Hans and his men returned safely to the settlement.

'I found Norse ruins but no Norsemen, my Gertrud', said Hans sadly to his wife, 'and though I am certain the district I have seen is where Erik and his men once lived I am more than ever convinced that the descendants of our countrymen will be found only on the eastern coast and that any attempt to reach it by land would be foolhardy indeed—even for your so often foolhardy husband!

'By sea round Cape Farewell will be the only way. Not in our boats, but in the native umiaks that are so light they can be carried over large stretches of ice and draw so little water they can sail close inshore behind the floes.

'One day it will be done, our countrymen found, but when is in the hand of God. And', his voice trembled a little, 'I do not think the finder will be Hans Egede, who is no longer a young man, and has now been given other sheep to feed'.

Fru Egede sat down and put her arm about him. She could find no words that seemed right for so bitter an occasion. They sat in silence for a little, then she got up and presently returned with a cup of steaming coffee and a glass of brandy.

'You are right, my husband', she said gently, putting them

down beside him, 'the time is in the hand of God. But this I shall say to everyone and to our children—especially to our child-dren, and one day it will be acknowledged, that *whoever* goes, it was Hans Egede—the man who obeyed a Voice—who first showed the way!'

Impulsively her husband caught her hands in his and held them fast. Then bending forward he kissed them and as he did so she felt his hot tears.

'Drink', she said softly, 'yes', as he glanced up at the brandy, smiled and shook his head. 'Yes, Hans, *both*!'

As so often, Gertrud Egede was right.

Though many attempts were made to reach the eastern coast it was not until over a hundred and fifty years later that an ex-pedition was successful in landing there; and its members trav-elled by sea—and in umiaks!

They found no Norsemen, only a small and rapidly diminish-ing colony of stunted, half-starved, eskimos. Had Gertrud Egede been alive she would, undoubtedly, have said the time had indeed been in the hand of God, her Hans spared so tragic a discovery....

What at the time seemed so complete a failure was not so. It will be remembered that the place where Erik-the-Red and his men first settled was called East Bygd and that later 'a second settlement grew up further north known as West Bygd'.

If you look at the map of Greenland you will see that West Bygd (which corresponds to the present Godthaab district), though considerably further north than East Bygd (the present Julianhaab area) lies well to the west of it. Hence its name and all the confusion caused by assuming East Bygd to be on the east and West Bygd on the west coast, when in reality both were on the west.

In the belief that he had discovered the western settlement, Hans had actually discovered the eastern, though it was many years before this was confirmed and he himself, as has already been said, was to die in the belief it lay on the east coast.

But he had not only discovered lost colonies. To Hans Egede, the poor, unknown clergyman from a remote country parish, goes the honour of having shown the way and the means by which Greenland's eastern coast that had baffled and defied so many over the centuries, would one day be reached.

122

More Downs than Ups

'Every complete devotion to an idea yields some profit, even though it be different from that which was expected', wrote Hans' great countryman Nansen; or, as Hans himself might have preferred to put it, 'God moves in a mysterious way'.

An insistent, compelling Voice had brought him to Greenland; yet he had not found those he had come to seek and now there was little certainty that he would do so.

Of one thing only he was sure; he had been given other sheep to feed. In those dark hours of defeat, frustration, and disappointment 'The Apostle of Greenland', as he was one day to be called, was born.

Hans Egede was to explore and colonise the country but it is as its Apostle, the man who brought Christianity to the Greenlanders, that he is best known today.

But there was no hint of this now. Only a dogged determination to increase and extend such teaching as he had already been able to give, and to do this without neglecting his trading work for the Bergen Company and the search for suitable places where small settlements or trading posts might be built.

One of the main reasons for this was to forestall the Dutch, who came in their whaling ships and who, although they had no right to do so in a Danish colony, set up small 'trading booths' as they were called where they exchanged Dutch goods for oil, furs and skins—all of which were consequently lost to the Bergen Company.

The chief whaling centre was in the area around Nepisat, 'six to eight days sailing time' from Delfsthaven, where Hans had gone the previous spring and, from what he had learnt then he felt sure Nepisat itself was probably the place where most of the trading took place.

His idea now was to visit this district and, if suitable, decide on a site for a small settlement.

As all building materials would have to be taken there, and any building completed and men installed before the first whaling ships arrived in early autumn he considered it was necessary to start as soon as possible in the new year, the first week in March at the latest.

In vain the old guide pointed out that it was far too early to venture so far north and he used a Greenlandic expression very like Fru Egede's favourite 'foolhardy'.

But Hans was adamant. Early or not he was going; the journey was essential. It was vitally important that trading was improved and the Dutch restrained. And he was not, he pointed out, proposing to travel in the frail native boats, but in stout Bergen yawls!

This time Fru Egede made no effort to dissuade him. She realised how necessary this journey was. She also knew from experience that when that look of stubborn determination appeared on his face it was better to remain silent, and though outwardly cheerful she went about her duties with a heavy heart.

Throughout most of February preparations for the journey went on and the month was barely over when the expedition, Hans himself, a mate, and eight men set out in two yawls.

Though bitterly cold the weather was fine when they started. A few snow-buntings, always the first harbingers of spring in the far north, had already arrived but except for their faint chirpings the land lay still and silent, blanketed deep in snow.

Sailing close inshore there were stretches of clear water where the sea-ice had begun to break up, but as they went further north these became daily more difficult to find; the floes larger and more dangerous; the cold more intense.

Heralded by flurries of blinding snow a north-easterly gale sprang up, lashing the sea to fury, and there was danger the boats might be swamped or damaged by the drifting floes. Finally a blizzard set in, making it impossible to see where they were going. Fortunately they had just reached Narsarmuit, a settlement of about sixty to seventy Greenlanders, and here they remained storm-bound for two days, sheltering as best they could under their boats which they managed to drag ashore.

When the storm eventually blew itself out and the sun emerged again, Hans took its altitude by means of a quadrant. It indicated a latitude of 65° 56′ North.

The interval of calm was short-lived; the sun soon disappeared and the wind began to rise again. The sky to the north looked sullen and thick with snow. This, together with the piercing cold, decided Hans against going further and on March 16th he gave the order to turn back.

In his diary he notes with regret not having reached Nepisat, which was only another two days' journey north, but by much questioning of the inhabitants of Narsarmuit he had managed to gather some of the information he needed.

Though the Dutch came there to trade, Nepisat, as he had thought, was the chief centre of their activities and here, he was determined, some kind of trading establishment must be built.

No details are given of the return journey, only that all arrived safely. That none of them was any the worse speaks well for their fitness and powers of endurance, especially when it is realised that they travelled in open boats, in temperatures far below Zero, and with few, if any, of the comforts, especially clothing, considered essential for travellers in these latitudes even in the decked and heated transport of today.

The heartfelt relief of Fru Egede when Paul and Niels, who had gone daily to the look-out rock, came shouting that the boats were in sight, can well be imagined.

As for the old guide, he stood smirking triumphantly and could be heard muttering something in Greenlandic corresponding to 'I told you so!'

It had been a courageous voyage but alas, the colonising of Nepisat was to prove an ill-starred venture.

From now on Hans began to concentrate vigorously on his missionary work. In not much more than two months the supply ships would arrive and reports, letters and matters of trade absorb most of his time.

Albert Top's enthusiasm for mastering Greenlandic was a great encouragement, and during the winter both of them had worked hard at it. Their chief difficulty now was not so much in ordinary everyday conversation but the impossibility of finding any Greenlandic words to correspond with abstract terms such as 'sin', 'blessing', 'holiness' used in Christian teaching. With visible things such as sheep or goats, corn or grapes, or even a loaf of bread, all so frequently mentioned in the gospels but which of course no Greenlander had ever seen, it was possible to rely on pictures and Paul was kept busy making drawings.

Among other things, Top, as he was now affectionately called, had persuaded Hans to allow a Greenland boy named Papa to live permanently at the settlement. Papa was as quick-witted and intelligent as Kusak but older and more reliable and was a great help to both men with the language.

In addition they had steeled themselves to live for short spells in the Greenlanders' winter houses taking this nauseating duty turn and turn about.

Though not nearly so strong a man, Top seemed better able to stand this experience than Hans, to whom the airless heat, the filth, and the smells, were always to remain little short of physical torture. Only because he believed it to be the best way of learning the language and of finding out how the Greenlanders' minds worked—what they actually thought and felt about things—could he bring himself to endure it.

Like the good countryman he was he was convinced it was necessary to clear the ground of weeds and stones before attempting to expect the gospel stories to take root. The weeds and stones in this case being the influence and teaching of the so-called soothsayers or angokoks; their 'devilish jugglery' as he sometimes described it.

He was anxious to make contact with the more important of these men but the angokoks seemed equally anxious to avoid the black-gowned, light-haired figure, with the keen blue eyes that seemed to pierce through them so accusingly. They were rarely seen but when they were their manner was furtive and defiant, often definitely hostile. That they were always lurking somewhere in the background exerting their sinister influence on their credulous countrymen Hans was certain. He also strongly suspected them of plotting and planning against Albert Top and himself.

An encounter with one of them came unexpectedly. On a short journey northwards to visit a summer camp, he spent the night with a Greenland family—a father, mother and several young children. The parents and children appeared healthy; judging from the amount of food stored in the tent the fishing and hunting were good; the family well-clothed and with all the meagre comforts available. But the father seemed sad and silent; the wife wept quietly but continuously, and the children wailed loudly at intervals. Even the tethered dogs suddenly broke into howls for no apparent reason.

126

It was all so unlike the usual cheerful Greenland household that Hans set himself to find the cause of the distress.

It appeared that a short while before an angokok had foretold the father would soon die, and as the children were too young to hunt and fish the little family was doomed to starve slowly to death.

Hans did his best to comfort the weeping wife and the wailing children, then he had a long talk with the father. God, he told him, He who was all-powerful and had made all men, He and He alone knew the allotted span of life, the hour of death for everyone.

The man seemed comforted and he smiled faintly when Hans promised to do his best to find the angokok who had foretold the disaster and punish him for his 'lying and deceit'.

The promise was fulfilled rather sooner than he expected for at another camp, on the return journey, Hans came face to face with the offending soothsayer.

In the presence of many Greenlanders he spoke so severely to him of his 'lying and apeing' and the distress and misery he had caused that the angokok was awed and 'abjectly acknowledged his witlessness'. Punishment too, is mentioned as having been meeted out; of what kind is not recorded, but it is safe to assume it was of the kind that Hans in his diaries sometimes refers to as 'a good beating' or 'a sound thrashing'.

Later generations have criticised him for this form of discipline but it must be remembered he was not only following the custom of his time, especially the strict ways of the Lutheran church at this period, when even erring parishioners were sometimes subjected to what was described as 'a little correction', but that he strongly suspected that he and his helpers might well be in danger of their lives from some of these men.

It was not long before these suspicions were realised. A little later, on a journey southwards, an encounter took place between the Trader from the settlement and an old angokok whom Hans had more than once rebuked for his 'conjuring tricks' as he called the spells and incantations used to influence the simple-minded Greenlanders.

As the Trader and his men came ashore from their boats they were met by a large number of Greenlanders.

Strutting up and down among them was the old angokok. He was armed with bow and arrows, and hung about with his full regalia of charms; beaks and claws of birds and other curious oddments. Suddenly, with threatening, menacing gestures he advanced towards the Trader who, fearing trouble, struck him on the jaw.

Enraged and scowling the angokok turned his back, retreated a little, then suddenly turned and prepared to shoot.

Before he could draw his bow the trader had levelled his gun at him. It was not loaded but this neither the angokok nor his fellow Greenlanders could know. What they did know however, was the terrifying power of the white man's hunting weapons and the rumours that they were not always confined to the slaughter of birds and animals. All, including the angokok, took to their heels and quickly disappeared into the nearby hills.

Later it was found that not only had the angokok plotted to murder the Trader and his men but was planning an assault on those left behind at the settlement.

As soon as this news reached Hans he took strict precautions.

Men taking it in turns kept a look-out by day; and others, armed with guns, watched for a surprise attack at night. The children were forbidden to go out of sight of the buildings.

In the fine summer weather this was a great deprivation and the boys especially grumbled continuously—so much so that Hans at last lost patience and threatened *them* with a beating.

As soon as the Trader returned from a short but necessary journey north, he and Hans, together with seven or eight men, set out southwards to search for the plotting angokok.

Without much difficulty he was found, brought to the settlement, his legs put in irons and 'a good thrashing' administered. He was then locked up, food brought him, and left alone to repent.

At the end of three days of wailing and entreating to be freed, and perpetually acknowledging his 'witlessness', he was released.

But a stern warning was given. From that day, he or any other 'caught again in that kind of rascality, would be unmercifully put to death'.

One or two more encounters with angokoks took place but their power was obviously waning. The Greenlanders were simple-minded but they were not fools. With their own eyes they had seen the hitherto terrifying power of their leaders wither before the calm, light-haired figure in the strange black garment—'the white angokok' as they now sometimes called Hans; with their own ears heard them acknowledge their 'witlessness'. The angokoks,

'd and New'—polar bear hunter from North
eenland and a worker from the boat-building
ds at Holsteinborg on the occasion of the
Royal visit of 1952.

Poek and Keperok. (Painting
by H. Grodtschilling in the
National Museum, Copenhagen)

North Greenland hunter and boy. (by V. Hansen)
'A hunter shoots his first seal before he is 10 years old.'

Illustrations from Hans Egede's book 'A new description of Greenland'.

Silver tankard presented to Hans Egede by his parishioners in Lofoten.

too, knew when they were beaten, and except for some half-hearted attempts at defiance from some of the younger ones, seem gradually to have disappeared from the scene.

With the teacher freed from threats of murder, and the taught from spells and misfortunes, the missionary work went ahead better.

Easy it could never be with such small and widely scattered groups, or constantly changing little companies coming and going and forgetting all they had been taught before contact could be made with them again. And there was always the discouragement: 'the luke-warmness' as Hans described it, after the first enthusiasm had worn off and any real effort at understanding or obeying his instructions was demanded.

Though many clamoured for baptism he had soon discovered this was by no means due to zeal for the Christian religion. For their children, so many of whom died in infancy as a result of their parents' ignorance or the harsh climate, it appeared to be regarded by many Greenlanders, as not infrequently happens even in Christian countries today, as a kind of insurance policy.

If 'the white angokok's' heaven was real, they reasoned, it was surely only prudent the baby should be given a chance to go there? There was also a certain social distinction to be gained. Courage, a virtue held in high esteem by all Greenlanders, was required to defy the threats of angokoks and also to brave the sometimes equally hostile disapproval of friends or relatives.

To the baptism of young children—'the babes' as he called them—Hans could usually be persuaded to agree, 'for of such is the Kingdom of Heaven'. Adult baptism was another matter and in regard to this he was adamant. Not only, he insisted, must it be preceded by promises of belief and reform but, particularly irksome to roving ways and minds, a period of instruction.

This question of instruction had been a difficulty from the very beginning, not only on account of the language, but the need and difficulty of keeping in touch with so widely scattered and frequently 'lukewarm' a flock. What so often happened was that once the Greenlanders had absorbed a few facts about the Christian religion and, the power of the angokoks now diminished or gone, abandoned one or two never very comforting beliefs, they considered that they had, so to speak, performed their side of the bargain.

To Hans and his assistants not only an infuriating but a very difficult situation to remedy!

The training of native 'catechists', Greenlanders specially selected and instructed who would live among and, under the supervision of the missionaries, teach their fellow countrymen, was agreed to be the best, indeed the only solution.

Among those selected for this training of whom a description has survived was the youth Papa already mentioned.

Papa was an extremely intelligent young man and well-liked by his fellow Greenlanders. He had been under instruction at the settlement for some time now and when the colonists were being selected to go up to Nepisat in charge of Albert Top it was decided he should go too and complete his training in practical work among the Greenlanders there.

In July, in glorious summer weather, the party of twenty-two, with a Greenlander to act as guide set out, followed by boats bringing building materials.

In one of these boats Hans, who had gone with them, returned to Hope Island.

He was well content. All, for once, had gone smoothly. Even before he left the building was already going ahead; the settlers, accommodated in tents, delighted with their surroundings; the friendliness of the Greenlanders; the amazingly prolific cod and salmon fishing; and full of the highest hopes for the trading.

In September the Trader and another four men were sent up and the returning boat brought the news that all were well; that few Dutch had been seen and none made any trouble, discouraged, it was confidently assumed, by the sight of the Danish flag flying bravely from the now completed little settlement house.

It was a confidence sadly misplaced. In the autumn, Greenlanders coming south brought disquieting rumours of fights and skirmishes with Dutch Skippers and whaling crews.

As early as possible the following spring Hans went up to see for himself. Though all at the settlement were well and cheerful he found the rumours had not been exaggerated and the news they gave him anything but encouraging.

Due to the condition of the ice that year the whaling had proved a miserable failure and the trade, which had apparently promised extremely well, had been snatched from under their very noses!

Frustrated by the whaling situation; furious at finding Norwegians and Danes in a place which by long established custom they considered their own, the Dutch had apparently lured away all the Greenlanders they could, bribing them with more and better goods than the colonists were able to offer for their skins and blubber.

In spite of everyone's optimism and assurance that they now knew the measure of the Dutch and would do better in future, Hans returned home troubled and discouraged. Later his anxiety was increased for in June of the same year the whole company arrived unexpectedly at Hope Island. Food, for some reason, had given out and they had returned, temporarily.

But they never went back. In August, while they were busy making preparations to leave, Greenlanders travelling down from the north reported that Dutch whaling skippers coming ashore and finding the little settlement house empty had set fire to it and burnt it to the ground.

As early as possible in the spring of 1726 men sent up to Nepisat confirmed this. Of the little, new colony nothing remained but smoke-blackened ruins.

Nailed to a charred beam was a notice. Written in bad Danish, signed by Dutch skippers, it threatened to kill anyone who interfered with their trade.

PART TWO

The year 1725 could hardly have been said to go well, but at least there was one happy event. On New Year's day the first baptism of an adult Greenlander had taken place; that of the young man Papa.

The ceremony was held at Hope Island and as travel from Nepisat would have been impossible so early in the year Papa had probably come down the previous autumn, though there is no record of this.

It was a joyful day at the settlement. 'Almost', as Petronella remarked, 'like Christmas!'

Though outside the wind shrieked and screamed, great gusts battering at the windows, and snow swirled this way and that in the murk and near darkness of the January day, inside the stoves glowed and there were flags and lighted candles.

All the previous day Fru Egede had been busy with extra baking, and among other delicacies waiting to be devoured were

131

plates piled high with dozens of the small sweet cakes particularly beloved by the Greenlanders.

For Hans it was a day of great happiness; a milestone in the history of the mission; his only regret that Albert Top had not been able to leave Nepisat to be present.

Papa—Frederik Christian as he was now called—was not only very intelligent but had worked hard and had done well in the little exam set him before his baptism. He could read and write some Danish now, and he was honest, reliable and very enthusiastic. Hans felt he would have no misgivings at sending him to work alone among his fellow Greenlanders. He also thought others might now be persuaded to come forward for training. And he was right; Frederik Christian was the first of many. Few at first, and not all of them a success, but slowly increasing down the years. Today over two centuries later, they have an important place in the flourishing church life of Greenland.

If things had gone badly in 1725 they seemed destined to go even worse in 1726. In the spring there was the sad confirmation of the fate of Nepisat. Hans had taken this so much to heart that even the thought of breaking the news when the ships from Denmark should arrive could cloud an otherwise happy day for him.

For the first time he was glad when May and most of June went by and neither had arrived. But early in July disquieting rumours began coming in and he reproached himself bitterly for his selfishness. Greenlanders travelling down from the north, Greenlanders travelling up from the south, all reported that never in living memory had such enormous quantities of drift ice been seen in Davis Strait so late in the year.

All through July anxiety grew for the safety of the ships. Two, three times a day, sometimes more, the children, their mother, members of the settlement, often Hans himself, would climb the look-out rock and stand scanning the horizon till their eyes ached.

The sun blazed down from a deep blue cloudless sky, hot enough, one would have thought, to melt any ice. But there it remained, the sea packed with it; great smooth blocks and small hummocky bergs glittering like diamonds. Some of these were quite near, grinding against the rocks and nearby skerries, caves scooped in their sides by the wash of the waves showing now blue, now emerald in the sunlight.

132

July gave place to August; still no ship had come and anxiety at the settlement increased every day.

The Egede children began to weary of going to the look-out rock; to be the first to sight a sail. The boys spent their time at the lake making the excuse that the more fish they could catch for salting should supplies fail to arrive, the better.

Petronella went with them. She never minded the writhings of newly caught fish or the handing out of messy bait; and, just occasionally, Paul would allow her to hold his rod for a little. One day she had 'nearly' as she proudly reported to Hans, 'caught a fish!'

'But not quite!' Niels contradicted scornfully.

Petronella scowled and her small fists clenched, began to walk threateningly towards him.

But Hans' nerves were on edge; this was no time for quarrelling children. He spoke so sharply to them that they both slunk away surprised and subdued and were quickly friends again.

Kirsten remained at home. She had always detested fishing and everything connected with it. And she had better things to do. Under her mother's guidance she was immersed in the intricacies of embroidery. Moreover, tomorrow would be her twelfth birthday . . . she was practically grown up. . . . She sat primly on a boulder shaded by a stunted willow, stitching away, her hands

hot and sticky and her fingers so swollen with gnat bites that she
could hardly hold the needle.

Deep down she was frightened. She was old enough to understand the sharp anxiety at the settlement and to sense something
of the horror a winter short of food—and possibly fuel—might
mean. She wanted to be at hand; to know immediately if a ship
was sighted.

Kirsten never forgot her twelfth birthday.

It was in the morning that the bad news came. Sitting with
her embroidery under the willow tree she saw her father, who

had stopped to talk to her, suddenly turn as white as the linen
in her lap as two breathless Greenlanders rushed up and spoke to
him.

Coming from the south they had seen a ship trapped in the ice
not far from land, men gathered on her deck waist-deep in water;
others in small ships' boats round about. As they stood watching
she began to sink and they could hear the cries of the men as they
jumped into the sea, and from those in the boats as these were
overturned or swamped; saw them for a time clinging to the
floes and calling; then only the ice and the sea—and silence.

There had been nothing they could do.

Even though strict rationing had now been imposed at the
settlement, stores, particularly grain, so essential to both man

and beast, were becoming dangerously low. Supplies of salted meat, game, and fish if quickly supplemented might be adequate but there would be nothing like enough grain to feed so many through the long winter.

August and the first days of September had now gone by and many openly expressed what all secretly feared : that the second supply ship had met the same fate as the first.

Fear, always catching, began to show itself in other ways; in impatience; in outbursts of anger; in incessant grumblings; all of which, Hans wrote later, he found even more distressing than the whole disquieting situation itself.

After much thought, prayer, and long troubled talks with Albert Top he called all at the settlement together. Under God, he told them, he was responsible for their welfare. The ship might yet arrive, equally she might not. With the present food stocks all were in danger, but with even four or five less to feed it might be just possible to survive the winter. One course and only one seemed open to him; to go north at once and try to persuade the next Dutch whaling skipper leaving for Bergen to take some from the settlement back with him.

To one still smarting from the hurt to Nepisat, the task Hans had set himself must have been particularly humiliating. That it was courageous probably never entered his head; only the stark fact that the lives of all at the settlement, including, of course, those of his own family, were at stake; that he had no other choice.

Later the same day, taking two men with him, he left for the north.

It had been a wonderful September; sunshine throughout the whole month; most of the drift-ice gone; new ice not yet formed.

One fine but windy day, not long before Hans' return, towards the afternoon the wind suddenly began to blow very much colder, almost a winter wind.

For some reason Fru Egede felt a strange urge to climb just once more up the look-out rock. Telling no one, she set off.

The wind, blowing from the sea, was against her as she climbed slowly and wearily; the weariness of one who has taken the same path many, many times, hoping against hope. Was it hope that had brought her here now? She hardly knew; only the strange, compelling urge to come.

Presently, a little breathless, she reached the summit, looked seawards. Sailing between the skerries, now rising, now dipping with the swell, white sails brilliant in the sunlight, billowing in the wind, was a ship—and at her masthead the Danish flag!

New Arrivals

PART ONE

Almost from the beginning the Bergen Company had realised that the meagre results of the trade with Greenland were going to be insufficient to pay their expenses. Though they expected matters to improve, for the present more money to run the Company must be forthcoming; the shareholders asked for further contributions. On the first occasion they agreed, grudgingly, but when further demands were made they stubbornly refused to contribute. Stormy scenes took place and many declared they were convinced that unless the King could be persuaded to assist them it would be necessary to give up the undertaking altogether.

It was finally decided to petition him to allow them a state lottery, a not unusual way of raising money at that time.

The petition was granted; other privileges were also conferred and the company continued its activities. But in 1724, of three ships sent to Greenland, one which had instructions to cruise along the eastern coast seeking a way through the drift-ice to the land, failed to return. Apart from the loss of life the loss of a ship was a serious matter; a bad and discouraging set-back for the Company. There were more stormy meetings. But in the autumn on board one of the other ships arriving at Bergen from Greenland were the accountant from the settlement and two young Greenlanders. One of these, Poek, had spent some time at the settlement receiving instruction from Hans and after much persuasion by the accountant had agreed to go with him to Denmark on condition he would be sent back the following spring.

Hans was particularly anxious for him to go. He thought the King's interest in Greenland would be stimulated by seeing one of its inhabitants, while Poek, on his return home, would be able to tell his fellow countrymen about life in a civilised country. It would also correct the idea, common among them, that Norwegians and Danes possessed neither land nor homes but were forever roaming about the sea! At the last moment he managed to persuade another Greenlander, Keperok, to go with Poek for companionship.

The day after their arrival in Denmark was the King's birthday and it was decided that as a surprise, the two Greenlanders should take part in the festivities arranged for the day. After being presented to the King at Frederiksborg Castle they gave a display of kayak-paddling and duck-hunting on the nearby lake.

The entertainment was a great success. No Greenlander had been seen in Denmark since 1654—the prisoners whose sad faces had so distressed Hans when he first saw their portraits. Later, when the 'Greenland procession'—a regatta on the canals surrounding Christianborg Castle—was held, Poek and Keperok took part, Copenhageners in their hundreds turning out to see them.

The enthusiasm was enormous. For weeks afterwards Greenland was the chief topic of conversation. There were illustrated pamphlets; ballads and sacred songs composed and printed. Ladies embroidered the procession in silk, and artists quarrelled for the privilege of painting the two Greenlanders' portraits. Neither trade nor mission could have had a better advertisement!

Early in the new year the King, 'inasmuch as his heart was moved by the Christian work undertaken by Hans Egede'—and also because he considered the continued navigation of Greenland of benefit to his subjects—increased the scope of the promised lottery.

Encouraged, the Bergen Company sent out two ships. But 1725 was the climax of their activities. With the loss of a second ship in 1726, disagreement among the directors and quarrels among the shareholders, it was clear the end of the Company was in sight.

Throughout the winter meetings were held in Bergen and Copenhagen to discuss the possibility of the Government taking over the trade completely. In the new year, at the command of the King, two ships were sent to Greenland to bring back full reports of the trading and other matters. But before they could return news of the destruction of Nepisat had reached Denmark.

The news caused great consternation among the King and his ministers. It was plain that not only were long established trading rights in Greenland in danger but Danish sovereignty itself being threatened. Stern action for the protection of both was necessary and urgent.

After much discussion it was decided that an expedition under the command of a Military Governor should be sent out.

Its purpose was carefully planned. Where necessary forts were to be built in the whaling and trading areas most frequented by the Dutch and other foreigners; help given to move the settlement from Hope Island to a new site on the mainland suggested by Hans Egede; and an expedition made to the eastern coast where, inhabited or not, it was firmly believed that large woods and precious metals would be found.

The Governor had orders to call together a council consisting of himself and members of the settlement to meet at least twice a week and deal with any disputes or difficulties that might arise. He, and all under him, were instructed to work for the 'preservation and propagation of the Christian faith;' to be careful of treating those at the settlement harshly and so making them unwilling to remain; and the 'savages'—meaning the Greenlanders—in such a way as to make them feel friendly towards the newcomers. The members of the council were to 'live in amity and mutual understanding and to show respect to one another'; the missionary work left strictly in the hands of the clergy.

Everything was most carefully considered, the King himself taking a deep interest in the whole matter, and personally expressing his best wishes for success to every member of the expedition before it sailed.

Hans was greatly heartened when the news reached him that a Governor had been appointed and troops would be sent out. After his return from Nepisat, Albert Top's health, never very good, had begun to fail badly. Arrangements had had to be made for him to go home in the spring and two young missionaries had been sent out to take his place.

His departure was a grief to all the Egede family. Hans, particularly, missed him greatly, and in spite of the fact that he now had two assistants instead of one, he found the combined worries of teaching his widely scattered flock and the Dutch-menaced trading more and more difficult. Both young men were able but training them in their duties took up time and neither was as proficient in the language as Albert Top had been on his arrival, or as quick to learn it.

But it was difficulties with the trading that worried Hans most at this time. The missionary work was bound up with it and if that failed the whole enterprise was in danger. A Governor with troops at his disposal would go a long way towards keeping the Dutch and other foreigners in their place.

Life in such surroundings could never be anything but hard but it did seem as if the long day to day struggle might now be eased a little; some leisure time available. An hour with a book; time to write a letter to a friend for 'posting' when next year's ship should come; a little leisure with his children. Children? They were children no longer! His sons were already young men. Later in the year Paul was to leave for the University in Copenhagen; while his daughters, he realised with a slight shock in which pride and sadness were mingled, were rapidly growing into young women; Kirsten, tall and graceful, her little plaits grown long but yellow and shining as ever, Petronella almost as tall, 'strong and sturdy as a little horse', as her mother sometimes remarked.

How would they compare with girls of their own age at home, he sometimes wondered? They were skilled in baking and brewing and all the household arts. Their mother had seen to that. They could knit, sew and embroider 'with the best' as she sometimes proudly said. Kirsten had a particularly sweet singing voice and both had made good progress with a spinet sent out one year by friends in Bergen. Their ordinary education, in spite of the many interruptions caused by his trade and missionary journeys was much as they would have received at home in Lofoten. Yes, they would hold their own he thought, but they would benefit from some contact with cultivated men and women of their own race, and he looked forward eagerly to the coming of the Governor and his staff, and the other new settlers.

But alas for hopes and plans! Early in July the ships from Copenhagen arrived and their passengers had hardly disembarked before it was clear that here were no peace-loving and cultured countrymen and women. Major Paars, the Governor, and his second-in-command, Captain Landorph, were obviously at loggerheads; later it was learnt they had quarrelled even before leaving Copenhagen, and so violently on the voyage that they had come to blows.

The strange truth was that in spite of all the care and thought given to the expedition, the Governor himself, his officers, and the majority of the troops and others under his command had been most unwisely chosen.

Though Major Paars was said by Hans Egede, who perhaps came to know all sides of his curious character better than anyone, to have many good qualities, they were certainly not those required by an efficient commander. Conceited, boastful, and altogether too full of his own importance, he was perpetually at odds with his officers, irresolute when decisions had to be taken, and unable to control the troops under him except by harshness.

Captain Landorph, though able, was a bad-tempered, jealous, and quarrelsome man; while the troops were mostly soldiers released from imprisonment for minor military offences, married to women freed from Copenhagen's jails and reformatories for the purpose, by the simple but barbarous method of drawing lots!

A small number of volunteers, for the most part respectable men and women, and a few young children completed the strange company.

The very next day after his arrival, with the bluster and bustle which characterised all his activities, Major Paars having hurriedly elected the necessary council as directed by the Government, commanded that he and the Captain of the ship that had brought him, be taken immediately to inspect the site on the mainland to which it was proposed to move the settlement, and if suitable decide whether it would be necessary to construct a fort there.

Accompanied by Hans and several of the newly-elected Council the party set out. The site was approved for building and for the rearing of cattle, a few of which had been sent out from Denmark in the last year or so, and though the Captain considered the entrance to the harbour difficult, the fact that it was a mile from the proposed settlement, no foreign ships ever seen there, and the natives friendly, the building of a fort seemed unnecessary.

Taking everything into account, it was decided to go ahead with the building immediately.

The following day a party of men in charge of an engineer was despatched to build a bakery, a brewery, and a small stone and turf hut as a temporary residence for the Governor. These completed, all energies were directed to the building of the settle-

141

ment house itself and the accommodation for the soldiers and other members of the expedition.

On August 20th, taking the name of the new settlement, Godthaab—meaning Good Hope—as his theme, Hans held his first service on the new site. What was one day to become the capital of Greenland was born!

So far, so good, but early in September torrential rain set in; rain heavier than any Hans had known since his arrival in the country. The tents where the troops and others were temporarily lodged were flooded out, the newly-erected hut for the Governor knee deep in water.

Trunks of clothes, chests of food and other stores were submerged, their contents soaked and much precious time wasted in digging ditches in the hard stony ground to carry off the water. The old settlement house on Hope Island, which for the past year or so had been anything but water-tight, now almost collapsed and the Egede family and many of the settlers took refuge in a warehouse, itself practically roofless with one side wide open to the weather.

Both the rain and the building went on relentlessly. It was essential to complete the houses before the cold set in, but insufficient building material had been provided which in turn meant insufficient accommodation, with the result that stores and goods of all kinds remained lying about exposed to the soaking rain.

The few horses brought from Denmark, already weakened by the long voyage, quickly died, so that in addition to the laborious work of blasting stone from rock some distance away, the men now had to carry it to the building site on their own backs.

This exhausting work, added to the heavy digging in the rocky ground, perpetually wet clothing—in which they slept in bedding equally wet, sapped their strength and their spirits. The food too was scanty and unsuitable, consisting almost entirely of salt meat which, together with the heavy work caused constant thirst.

There was no shortage of water but the beer ration soon gave out. When this happened, Major Paars who alternately bullied and cajoled his men into speeding up the work, replaced it with one of spirits which, much to Hans' disapproval, was constantly increased.

By Sunday, September 19th, the rain had eased a little and in the midst of damp and discomfort a short dedication service took place, the rest of the day being recorded as having been celebrated 'with the requisite moderate gaiety'.

By the end of the month the buildings were more or less completed and on September 30th Fru Egede thankfully supervised the removal of the family belongings from the damp and draughty warehouse to the new long, low, one-storied house which was to house the Egede family as well as the Governor, Captain Landorph, and the two missionaries. The rest of the officers, six in all, were accommodated in a kind of loft under the rafters, cramped for space, sparse of light and bitterly cold.

Later Major Paars built a small battery outside his windows consisting of seven guns brought from Hope Island, and erected a white painted flag staff from which the Danish flag was to be flown on high days and holidays.

Before the completion of the new buildings Paul had left for Copenhagen. Unlike their usual talkative selves the Egede family walked back in silence from the look-out rock where they had gone to wave their last farewells.

Each was immersed in his or her thoughts. Hans was reminded of his own first departure from home, the long, lonely voyage . . . how much lonelier a departure was this! . . .

Except for the rare chance of a letter sent or received by a passing whaler nearly a year must go by before they could even hear if this much loved and loving son had arrived in safety or he receive news of them. . . . In the matter of scholarship he had few misgivings; Paul was a sound Latinist—he had seen to that—his Greek very fair, and other subjects mostly good. . . . Fortunately too, he had been old enough before they left Bergen to remember life in a civilised country; Copenhagen would not be too woefully strange to him, and they had many friends there. . . .

Kirsten wept silently; Petronella less restrainedly; the days when Paul would pick her up and carry her under his arm 'like a parcel' were long past, but, Paul was Paul, and she loved him very much!

Niels walked alone, a little ahead. Though always sturdily independent he relied in many ways on this less than a year older but always so much wiser brother. He was going to miss him greatly. They had had long talks together these last few weeks. . . .

Fru Egede walked with her arm in Hans', her face pale and

set. Not until they were alone together that evening did she break down. Three, possibly four, years must go by before she could see this first born son of hers again. Fru Egede was a strong woman but over seven years of incessant toil in the hard Greenland climate had tried her strength; she was thirteen years older than Hans and no longer a young woman.

Three years . . . Four years . . . A cold fear, a sudden foreboding of disaster swept over her as she clung weeping to Hans confiding these fears. Hans did his best to comfort her but again he was reminded of his own home-leaving—his aged and ailing father, and a shadow passed over his face as he spoke tenderly to his usually steadfast and self-controlled wife, reminding her, among other things, that they still had Niels at home, adding, with an attempt at a laugh, that *he* showed no sign of wishing to leave them for a university career!

It was true. But though Niels had no academic leanings, he had other talents. Both he and Paul had long since won the Greenlanders respect for mastery of their language, which both now spoke as readily as Norwegian. In addition, Niels was respected for his mastery of their kayak.

It was Kusak who, in the spring after Niels' thirteenth birthday, had yielded to his pleadings and agreed to teach him this very difficult art.

Never had there been a more patient teacher; a more impatient pupil! Continually, furiously, Niels rebelled against the exacting discipline required. He was so sure he could learn more quickly his way!

'There is only *one* way', Kusak would insist with infuriating calm, '*our* way. Your way, you never be good kayaker.'

And, scowling with frustration, teeth chattering with cold, Niels would seize the paddle and the lesson start all over again.

'Kusak has far more patience than I!' said Hans to Fru Egede one day after witnessing a lesson. 'And Niels, who can't—or won't—persevere ten minutes with a piece of Latin prose will concentrate on a kayak lesson till he is too cold to speak!'

Sometimes Kusak would recall those days. 'You very slow to learn, not like Greenland boys! But now', he would add handsomely, 'you good as a Greenlander—*almost.*' At which tribute, however cold he might be outwardly, Niels would glow within.

As so often occurs in families when an elder brother or sister leaves home, the next in age appears to step into his or her shoes.

144

With Paul's departure this now happened to Niels. He seemed suddenly to become older, more thoughtful, more responsible.

There was plenty of scope for it! As winter began to close in it was evident that everything was far from well at the newly-built and now completed settlement, and all Hans' hopes for a little peace and leisure melted away like snow flakes in spring.

Now that the building was finished and winter set in Major Paars and his officers had too little to do. They bickered and quarrelled incessantly and were frequently drunk; hardly an example to the already ill-disposed and unwisely chosen men and women under them, whose behaviour was such that even the Greenlanders were shocked and expressed doubts as to whether the white man's religion made men any better.

Hans was greatly distressed. Such a state of affairs was no advertisement for the Christian faith, and only helped to undermine his missionary work. His time, too, was constantly wasted at the council meetings where important decisions were invariably put on one side and trivial matters argued about, sometimes for an entire day, so that by November he had asked to be excused from attending them.

As the weather became colder there was growing resentment and discontent among the soldiers; so much so that the council began to fear a mutiny. There were disquieting rumours; a sergeant when drunk was said to have sworn to kill both Hans and the Governor.

Hans was the chief centre of animosity. But for him, it was argued, none of them would have been sent to this cursed country.

Throughout the seven and a half years spent in Greenland, except for accidents and minor illnesses, the health of the settlers had been remarkably good. Now, as the cold increased, serious illness thought to be principally scurvy broke out, and with alarming suddenness death was among them striking right and left.

At first it was chiefly the newcomers who were attacked, but very soon the disease spread to the whole colony including those in the ships wintering in the harbour.

Whenever possible parties were sent out to search for scurvy grass, but whether this was insufficient or whether the illness, which attacked weak and strong, young and old alike, was not really scurvy, it remained unchecked and the unsuitable food, dirty bedding and habits of most of the newcomers did little to keep it from spreading.

As the surgeon who had come with the expedition dryly remarked 'with such conditions things would have been the same even if each patient had had a doctor and dispensary to himself'.

By the end of the year twenty-eight people had died. By February most of the survivors were so weak they were unable to dig graves in the hard rocky earth, and the dead, sewn into hammocks, were taken to the hut used temporarily by the Governor on his arrival, to await burial in the spring.

Throughout this period of distress private journals and the records of the Council show how futile were the Governor's attempts at discipline, how unedifying the behaviour both of himself and those under him.

To banish thoughts of the danger which lurked among them, and perhaps to avert attention from his own quarrels, Major Paars was constantly arranging festivities of one kind or another. These invariably ended in drunkenness or rowdyism of some kind.

On one occasion a violent quarrel broke out between himself and Captain Landorph. The captain, described as 'excessively drunk', after having used extremely abusive language, suddenly seized his superior officer, tore off his wig, trampled on it, and throwing him across a bed, beat him black and blue. When the ill-treated Governor recovered he declared his attacker under arrest, at which the Captain only laughed and shrugged his shoulders, and whether the Governor thought better of it, or was unable to enforce the order, remained free. The incident, however, can hardly have endeared them to each other!

As the year neared its end, reports and journals show very clearly the state of fear and misery to which the settlement had been reduced.

'Towards Christmas', wrote Johan Fleischer, the supervisor of stores, 'it was discovered that some of those released from prisons and sent to Greenland had conceived a plan to kill the Governor, the good old clergyman, Hans Egede, and others. This frightened us all so much that the Captain, the clergymen, and all the officers took turn to keep watch. Nay, we were in such great fright that none of us dared leave our abode without being armed'. And he adds that when the clergy took the sacrament to the dying 'they dared not do so without carrying a pistol under their cassocks.'

As the weather grew warmer, however, the disease gradually began to subside. Early in April the last deaths occurred; those of a little girl who had come with the skipper of one of the ships, and another small child. Most of the survivors attended this last sad little funeral. Altogether no less than forty-six people had died.

April 16th was the Queen of Denmark's birthday, an occasion promptly seized upon by Major Paars for very special festivities.

Though reports state that 'everyone of importance was invited', such was the general dislike and disrespect in which the Governor was held that very few—the Egede family among them—accepted the invitation, the majority preferring to attend a celebration on one of the ships.

Though Hans is known not to have disapproved of either wine or spirits in moderation, and sometimes enjoyed taking part in a friendly bout of wrestling, it has been considered a little surprising that he attended—and allowed his young family to attend these rowdy and riotous gatherings. That he did so himself was probably more out of respect for the Governor's position than the Governor, and with the prevailing rumours he may well have considered his family safer under his eye.

Whatever the reason, there is no doubt that he strongly disapproved of the way the entertainments were conducted for it is recorded that he 'frequently rebuked' the Governor for his behaviour—'once going so far as to refuse him communion'.

With the fine spring weather and the melting of the snow, Major Paars was all agog to carry out one of the principal tasks allotted to him, an overland expedition to the east coast 'by way of The Iceberg' as he was pleased to describe the unexplored and forbidding Inland Ice.

Hans, who can have had little, if any, faith in the expedition, gave what information he could, advising the party to travel by boat to the head of Amerilik fiord and then on foot to the edge of the ice; from there the Governor to decide for himself what to do next.

Full of self-importance and in the highest spirits; accompanied by seven men and two Greenlanders to act as guides; with guns and ammunition, and provisions for eight days, Major Paars set out.

From the full and very graphic descriptions which he wrote of his journey it appears that after leaving their boats he and his men 'walked for two days in a leisurely manner' through a rocky valley, arriving at noon on the third day at the edge of the Inland Ice 'and in danger of my life attempted to advance across it'.

Very soon, however, the party was halted, huge deep crevasses blocking the way, 'steep and sheer as the sides of a church' while the Ice Cap itself, 'The Iceberg' as he persisted in calling it, he describes as looking 'like the wild ocean when no land is to be seen'; its surface 'sharp-edged like white sugar candy'.

It was enough. Abandoning any attempt to penetrate further he ordered a salute of nine guns to be fired. This done, he and his companions 'sat down on the ice, and in a glass of spirits drank the health of our most gracious King, an honour which until then had never befallen The Iceberg!'

The celebration over they set out on their return journey.

They chose a different route this time, actually that taken 160 years later by the explorer Nansen when in 1888, with four companions he made the famous 'first crossing of Greenland', travelling on skis across the Ice Cap from the east coast to the west.

On May 5th 'after a fateful and very arduous passage' all the party returned safely to the settlement.

Today Major Paar's 'Ascent of the Iceberg' as he grandly called it, would be considered a very mild achievement, but at the time it was important; an attempt to penetrate beyond the margin of the Inland Ice and confirmation of what was already suspected—the grim and dangerous nature of its surface.

The east coast, however, was no nearer, and though thankful to see the expedition return in safety, Hans must have smiled to himself!

PART TWO

All through May the fine spring weather continued and Major Paars in his boisterous way would slap 'good Mr. Hans', as he had taken to calling him, on the back and declare Greenland was not such a bad place after all!

He was full of impatience to fulfil the third of the tasks allotted him, the establishment of buildings and a fort at Nepisat, and very soon after the return from 'The Iceberg' men were sent ahead

148

to start preparations. Captain Landorph and himself, having apparently patched up their quarrels, following with Olë Lange, the younger of the two missionaries, at the end of the month.

They arrived on June 10th and soon after were joined by one of the ships that had wintered at Godthaab bringing stores and a whaling crew; in all seventy-six people.

The work of unloading the ships, quarrying stone, and cutting turf for fuel went ahead quickly in the long June days. Very soon the actual building was begun, a fair-sized dwelling house, and, a short distance from it, a big warehouse.

The uneasy truce between the Governor and his second-in-command was soon at an end and they quarrelled unceasingly.

Though Captain Landorph and Johan Fleischer, the supervisor of stores, were usually hostile to each other, they would immediately join together against the Governor in any dispute. In his own words 'insulting him grossly . . . mocking him . . . depriving him of the love and goodwill of his officers'.

Though the warehouse was completed by the end of the summer the dwelling house did not look like being habitable for some time and Major Paars, who liked his comforts, announced his intention of returning to Godthaab to spend the winter 'with good Mr. Hans', a decision privately celebrated with great glee by officers and men alike. On September 3rd he was back at Godthaab.

For some time now Hans had been concerned about Niels's future and all his prayers for guidance seemed unanswered. The boy would soon be eighteen . . .

'You must be content with *one* scholar in the family', said Fru Egede when he discussed the matter with her. 'Niels has always been an outdoor boy—from a tiny child he has disliked being within four walls.'

Reluctantly Hans agreed. But there was not much scope here in Greenland. The official Trader would be leaving next year, perhaps as his successor the boy might do well?

Niels himself seemed pleased with the idea. Though he had often been with his father and others on their bartering expeditions, to be in charge of one himself was a very different matter! He set about learning more of the work with zest and looked forward to pitting his wits against Dutch and Englishmen. But not long after Paul's departure, greatly to his father's surprise, he suddenly began to take a deep interest in the missionary work as well.

At first Hans thought it was a passing enthusiasm but it soon became evident his son was in earnest. Unlike himself with his imperfect and halting Greenlandic, Niels spoke the language perfectly. He also understood the Greenlanders' ways far better.

'I know how they *feel*, Father', he insisted. 'And I know I could make converts.'

Willingly, but still doubtful whether Niels would show any real aptitude for the work, Hans took him with him on his next christening journey. At the end of a week he acknowledged Niels was right. He really did seem to know how the Greenlanders felt, and there was no doubt he was very popular with them, both young and old. It was not only that he spoke their language; he also sang their songs and played their games; he wore the same clothes; above all he had mastered their kayak, and was a skilled hunter.

His prayers, Hans realised, had been answered, if rather differently from the way he had expected. This strong, sturdy young man would have opportunities as a Trader to carry the gospel message far and wide, to sow its seed in places he himself could never hope to reach. But, grateful as he was, he could not help smiling a little at the thought of Niels, from childhood so independent, so disobedient—even defiant—and so very loath to learn from books, as a missionary!

'He will do well, you will see', murmured Fru Egede, a faraway look in her eyes, as if she could already see the future; the love and honour, the recognition by country and King that would some day come to this outdoor son of hers.

Meanwhile, at the ill-starred Nepisat things were not going well. The whaling, on which so much depended, was a complete failure. Not a single whale, as Major Paars was later to report, was seen, much less caught! Such building as could be done in the intense cold went on but the work was hard and the food poor. Many fell ill with scurvy and before the winter was over seven men had died.

The return of spring brought some improvement. It also brought Major Paars, and quarrels and disputes again became the order of the day.

By mid-summer the dwelling house was completed and two

batteries erected but the fort, so necessary for the protection of the whole enterprise, was still not built, Major Paars being unable to agree with Captain Landorph about a suitable site.

The short summer was now at an end and although there was fish in plenty and berries for the picking, food and fuel stocks were low and other stores dwindling; supplies expected from Godthaab failed to arrive and it began to be feared that the ship from Denmark had been lost. Soon it was obvious to everyone there would not be enough to feed so many through the winter.

No whales; no fort; shortage of food; shortage of fuel. So, roughly, ran Major Paar's report to the authorities in Denmark. In consequence, there being no use for their services, he was sending back the whaler, her crew, and all the soldiers.

As he stood watching their departure, his bluster and bravado for once must have forsaken him. In the most important part of his mission, the protection of the Greenland trade by force of arms, he had failed miserably. Without doubt, as soon as the news reached Denmark he would be recalled. . . .

The winter was setting in abnormally early; return to Godthaab and 'good Mr. Hans' in small open boats—the only transport left him—was impossible. He was faced with the prospect of a winter short of food, short of fuel, shut up alone with his enemies.

Winter was indeed setting in early. Even in August there were flurries of snow and at Godthaab, though the sea round about never froze completely, patches of ice were already beginning to form. Here too there was concern for the second of the year's supply ships, the *Morianen,* scheduled to leave Copenhagen on May 22nd. Towards the middle of August hope of her arrival had been almost abandoned but early on the morning of the 22nd she was sighted.

As soon as she reached the nearby islands Hans rowed out to her, the boat cracking and splintering the thin ice, and held a thanksgiving service on board for her safe arrival; she had been three months on the voyage, beset by storms, mountainous seas and contrary winds.

Hans had additional cause for thanksgiving. Among her papers the ship had brought orders from the King recalling Major Paars and his troops!

August 20th was now laid down as the very latest date for ships to start the return journey with safety, so that even in a normal year her captain would have had no choice but to winter in Greenland.

It was late, too, for sailing north and with ice already forming he dared not take the risk. Nepisat must hold out as best it could; the letters for the Governor wait until the spring . . . and he prepared to settle in for the winter.

Meanwhile the Greenlanders had moved into their winter houses and Hans was kept busy going from one settlement to another, both on the mainland and the islands, sometimes as far as Baals river, baptising small children as he had promised earlier in the year.

In the first week of October, however, snow, heavier than any he had known since he landed in the country, set in. Birds and animals died and on the wintering ship many of the crew fell ill with scurvy. Supplies of scurvy grass, already scanty that year, became impossible to find in the deep snow, and several men died.

Illness of some kind also broke out among the Greenlanders, spreading rapidly in their overcrowded, overheated and ill-ventilated houses.

Between the blizzards Hans battled through the deep snow or rowed in and out of the ice visiting the sick or taking the sacrament to the dying. Sometimes Niels went with him and the two of them, caught in a blizzard and refusing shelter with the Greenlanders for fear of infection, often spent a day, and sometimes a night as well, wrapped in blankets, but still shivering, in the shelter of their upturned boat on some small wind-swept skerry. Meanwhile at the settlement snow drifted higher every day and Fru Egede and her daughters watched in turn through a little circle (made by putting a hot coin against the frozen window pane) for their coming.

In the ship scurvy seemed to be abating though the men were still weak, but well into December disease continued to ravish the Greenlanders and Hans was saddened at the deaths of so many young children some of whom he had only recently baptised.

Towards the end of the month, however, all had recovered and Niels, desperately anxious to show what he could do to improve the trading, was able to visit their homes for bartering, taking all the men he could with him.

Writing in January, which he describes as the coldest period he has yet spent in Greenland, Hans complains he is left with only one man at the settlement making it impossible for him to leave it, but adding he was prevented from doing so in any case owing to the deplorable state of his footwear. This apparently was so bad that he writes, 'There was no possibility of getting about, and my time was uselessly wasted'.

Wasted as far as the missionary work was concerned perhaps, but hardly 'wasted', for he apparently spent the enforced leisure trying to work out a better system of barter.

Until now the Greenlanders had simply pointed at the goods they wanted and produced skins, blubber and walrus tusks in amounts they considered a fair exchange. Both sides then added or subtracted until a satisfactory bargain was arrived at. To improve on this rough and ready arrangement was not easy, and Hans found it particularly difficult in regard to blubber which he describes as liquid in summer and sold by measure, but in winter frozen solid, caked with snow and ice and sold by weight!

The spring was very slow in coming and not until late in May would the Captain of the *Morianen* venture north to Nepisat, even then only arriving after 'three weeks of very hard sailing'.

Hans, who had matters to discuss with the Governor, was on board and the ship had hardly anchored before he received the saddening news brought by a newly arrived Dutch whaler that the King of Denmark had died the previous October.

It was a bitter blow. Hans had a personal affection for the King who had not only shown him much kindness but also been partly responsible for bringing him to Greenland.

But worse was to follow. A few days later a Danish ship, not finding him at Godthaab arrived at Nepisat in search of him.

She brought urgent despatches from the new King, Christian VI. All, both at Nepisat and Godthaab, were commanded to return to Denmark 'with the exception of Hans Egede who might stay through the winter on certain conditions'.

It was shattering news!

'For me', wrote Hans not long after receiving it, 'it was very grievous tidings, and it went to my heart as nothing else in the world could have done . . . that all the diligence and labour put into the teaching of these poor ignorant people should be wasted and in vain.'

153

He goes on to say how unwilling he was to leave the country on account of 'the poor Greenlanders', especially the children he had baptised, some 150—'who lay as much at my heart as ever children could lie at the heart of a loving mother.'

As to his remaining alone in the country 'every right-minded Christian' must realise it was utterly impossible unless he was allowed helpers, sufficient provisions, and the assurance of future assistance by the King.

At the first opportunity, 'in great trouble and distress of mind' he returned to Godthaab.

Fru Egede had been ill in his absence and under the circumstances Hans thought she might well be glad to leave Greenland with all its toil and hardships. But she expressed no pleasure at the prospect; only grief for his grief; sorrow at the thought of leaving those whose lives and teaching were now his chief care; a land and a people who had come to mean so much to all the family.

12

'Night shall be thrice night over you . . .'

'. . . Night shall be thrice night over you
And heaven an iron cope,
Do you have joy without a cause,
Yea, faith without a hope ? . .'

PART ONE

So wrote the poet G. K. Chesterton nearly two hundred years later, but it might well have expressed Hans' feelings, indeed those of the whole Egede family, during the next few years.

At Nepisat everything that could possibly be moved was hurriedly loaded on to the waiting ships. Only the empty buildings, a half-finished boat, some rough wooden crosses marking the shallow graves of those who had died, remained. Later in the year the Dutch were to burn and destroy all the buildings. Soon the wooden crosses would rot and fall; grass in summer, snow in winter cover the shallow graves; the ill-fated colony be nothing but a name and a memory.

Soon after the ships arrived at Godthaab on July 12th, 1731 a meeting of the Council was called; the King's orders read and discussed.

To abandon the missionary work was agreed by all to be indefensible. It was also considered impossible to leave the settlement buildings and merchandise unprotected. The ships were already heavily loaded and could carry little more. Left to itself the settlement house, the sheds, warehouse, and all they contained would be at the mercy of the Dutch and other foreigners; raided; burnt; Danish links with the country weakened, or possibly broken for ever. Hans Egede had been told he might, if he wished, remain in the country until the spring. If he did so wish, and could persuade any to stay with him, they, the Council, had orders to allow up to ten men to do so.

As Hans sat listening, torn between hope and despair, he was reminded of meetings in Bergen . . . in Copenhagen . . . of a little sandy beach, and a Voice that urged insistently. Was the work of over twenty years to be undone by an apparently indifferent King, incompetent officials, and merchants impatient for profits? His face as he stood up to reply was stubborn; his formidable jaw thrust forward, and his blue eyes particularly piercing as he glanced round at the assembled councillors. The King's letter, he said, had given him 'the opportunity to get away from the wilds of Greenland', and had it been only a question of his own and his family's welfare he might have agreed, but his conscience would not allow him to leave those who had 'developed a taste for the sweet and blissful words of God'. He and his family were prepared to remain, but only if volunteers were forthcoming could they do so, the missionary work be carried on, the settlement and its property protected.

There was silence for a moment after he sat down; then the Council agreed that all the settlers should be called together, everything fully explained and volunteers asked for.

While they waited for everyone to assemble, Niels, who had been sitting perched on a window-sill at the side of the room, came and sat down by his father. He knew well what this hour must mean for him—and hardly less for himself, his mother and sisters.

Hans sat silent, but glancing at him Niels noticed that the stubborn look had left his face. His eyes were no longer piercing. They had 'a comfortable blue look' as Scot said of his friend Dr. Wilson in the Antarctic. It was a look with which many sick Greenlanders were familiar—and many more so soon to know. His anxiety and indignation seemed suddenly to have left him, given place to a calm confidence.

Niels himself felt anything but confident. Several of the most steadfast of the settlers had told him how the recent harsh winter and the outbreaks of serious illness had daunted them. Many whom he thought might otherwise have agreed to stay had already arranged to leave; others, the two missionaries among them, held four-year appointments and were under orders to return.

All who could be found had now arrived. There was much whispering and murmuring and scraping of chairs on the bare boards; then the Governor rose to speak and a hush fell on the hot, overcrowded room.

When all had been explained there was a short silence, then the murmurings and whisperings broke out again.

Now volunteers were being called for . . .

Niels did not dare to look at his father. Texts from the Bible jostled confusedly together in his mind. 'Who is on my side—who?' 'If ten just men be found?'

Now there was a shuffling of feet and four out of the seven Bergen men living at the settlement thrust up their hands and announced they would be willing to stay. They were quickly followed by four of the crew of the *Morianen*. A short pause, and then two carpenters, men who had been at the settlement from the beginning, stood up. They would leave when Hans Egede did they said stoutly, and not before! Another man, two men, began to speak but the Governor held up his hand. Ten! The Government had agreed to provide for ten, and ten only . . . Any others who remained would have to provide for themselves!

There was another short silence. Niels and his father turned and looked at each other but it seemed to Niels that Hans did not really see him at all—that he looked far beyond him to some distant place—some Heaven of thanksgiving that he alone could see. . . .

But now the Governor was speaking again. Slowly Hans turned his head and gave his attention. Directly the speech was over he was on his feet, brisk and alert, once again an organiser and a man of action.

After thanking those who had agreed to stay with him he asked that two requests might be granted. Firstly, in case the ship sent to fetch him might not arrive, that stores for two years be left him. In return for these he would give any profits from the trade towards the extra cost, and should no Danish ship arrive before the end of the second year, see to it that any such profits and all remaining stores and goods be sent back by a foreign ship. Secondly, he asked that his son Niels, now acting as Trader, should be officially elected. Both requests were agreed to and soon after the meeting broke up.

'Thus was I relieved of my anxiety', he wrote, ending an account of it later in his diary. 'And for this, after God, I have to thank those good men who so faithfully, by word and deed, have stood by me'.

Time was getting short before the ships were due to sail. Selection of what was most needed by the remaining settlers had to be made, and lists of all goods and Government property left behind carefully listed.

Like a good countryman Hans began with the animals.

'*Fourteen* barrels of oats—for these few beasts!' objected Johan Fleischer who was in charge of the stores.

'Fourteen', replied Hans firmly. 'Undernourished cows produce sickly calves and poor milk!' He was also particularly careful about the seeds he needed, and a list of these still survives. 'Peas and beans; turnips; horse-radish; spinach; sage and chives; asparagus and parsley.'

On July 24th the first ship sailed; three days later the *Morianen* weighed anchor. On board her stood Major Paars, the first, and for many years the last Governor of Greenland.

Rowing back with his family from Hope Island where they had gone to wave their goodbyes, his shoulders still aching from the Governor's hearty farewell slaps, Hans was chiefly aware of an enormous sense of relief. Only those dedicated to the country and its welfare now remained. In all about twenty people including himself and his family. A tiny handful in a vast, barely known land.

PART TWO

By the returning ships Hans had sent back reports with a full account of his activities over the last ten years and imploring the King's support for continuing the mission. As for the poor trading results, he was confident they could be greatly improved if certain suggestions of his were carried out.

There was no doubt these reports made a great impression on the new King and brought about a surprising change of heart. Later, a meeting with Olë Lange whose fervent support for continuing the missionary work and concern that Hans Egede, 'that right-minded servant of God, with his indefatigable zeal for the spreading of the Christian gospel, should be comforted in his anxiety' decided him.

He acted quickly. A letter was sent to the head of the Navy instructing him and members of the Missionary College to discuss with some 'level-headed merchants' how best to assist 'both the cause of Christianity and the trade in Greenland' and a promise to consider his support for both.

At the same time a meeting of the former council in Greenland was called at which Major Paars, the quarrelsome Captain

158

Landorph, Olë Lange, the chief Trader, and others were present.

Hans' proposals for a new settlement at Disko Bay which, rightly, it was to prove, he considered the most important place for trading, were discussed; Major Paars, who had barely mentioned the matter in his reports home and had certainly never given Hans any credit for the suggestion, loudly applauding the idea. He also repeated a previous suggestion of his own; the setting up of small settlements or trading stations every twenty-five miles or so from Cape Farewall in the south to Umanak fiord in the north.

In this way, he declared, the country would be well-guarded and the missionary work prosper, for nearly everywhere the Greenlanders would meet clergymen 'so that they could not escape from them', as he curiously expressed it!

He also considered his scheme would frustrate the Dutch who would arrive to find the Greenlanders had bartered everything to the Danes 'and would therefore, in future, remain at home'.

Further meetings took place at which ship owners and 'level-headed merchants' were present.

Among these was Jacob Severin, a leading Copenhagen merchant, a man of forceful character, determination, and integrity who was to play an important part both in Hans' life and the whole future of Greenland.

He had great faith in Hans and thought that the missionary work could, and should, go on, though like all the other merchants he was unsure of the success of the trade. He was, however, prepared to consider taking it over, remarking dryly that 'throughout history there could seldom have been a more honest and Christian one!' Many more meetings took place; two other merchants agreed to support him, but then withdrew.

It was a big risk for one man to take alone and Severin was unwilling to agree to it without further information. Finally he decided to send ships at his own expense the following spring to bring him back a fuller report.

While all these discussions were going on in Copenhagen Hans and the tiny band of colonists left behind at Godthaab went about their daily work.

In the months immediately following Major Paars's departure things had gone very well. The weather had remained exceptionally fine; well into November, though very cold, no heavy snow had fallen and Niels was able to carry on trading expeditions both to the north and south, returning each time with his boat loaded with blubber.

Hunting expeditions he arranged for other members of the settlement did well too and before the end of the year Hans could report that he had accomplished more by the energy and enterprise of his son than with the two former Traders together.

The blubber alone was more than in any previous year—135 barrels of it already stored and ready to be sent home! And in his carefully kept accounts he also lists '3 barrels of spermaceti' (a kind of wax from the heads of sperm whales), '190 seal skins; 263 fox-skins; 43 reindeer hides; and 47 pieces of whale bone'.

But when Niels and the hunting parties were away—sometimes there was only one man left at the settlement—Hans had to deal with the bartering of any skins that might come in and with the weighing and packing of the blubber into barrels. In this he was joined by Fru Egede who handed over some of her household duties to her daughters in order to help him.

Hard, nauseating work at the best of times, once winter set in it became almost unendurable. The draughty warehouse was unheated and the health of both husband and wife suffered badly from the cold, Fru Egede's more seriously than was realised at the time.

Though he always held the Sunday and feast days services this bartering and blubber-weighing was a constant interruption to Hans' own work and prevented him from making journeys to his widely scattered flock, but whenever he could he snatched time to visit Greenlanders living near the settlement, reading to them, and instructing those already baptised.

The catechist Frederik Christian was a great help at this time, often making boat journeys to small settlements on the outlying islands and staying with the Greenlanders in their winter houses. Born and brought up in one the dirt, heat, smells, and general discomfort so distressing to Hans, went unnoticed by him, and though he was unable to teach he spent many happy hours reading to his countrymen and to their children.

The end of November, however, brought the tardy arrival of winter. Severe frosts and heavy falls of snow quickly put an end to the trading and hunting expeditions. Hans was able to leave the settlement and in spite of bitter cold managed to make several boat journeys.

Everywhere, he wrote, parents brought their small children to him, begging him to baptise them, but with the uncertainty of whether or not he was to stay in the country and be able to continue teaching he had sadly to refuse.

The Greenlanders could not understand why the king wished him to leave. If it was a question of food, they insisted there were enough reindeer, seals, fish, and birds to feed the very small number now at the settlement.

'We know you are fond of us', they added, 'or you would have left us last summer, like all the others!'

In January, normally one of the coldest months, the weather became almost warm; 'so extremely beautiful', Hans describes it, 'that it could have been anywhere in a northern country at this time of year . . . the air mild and soft, almost spring-like'.

The cold, however, soon returned and almost up to mid-summer the weather remained unusually changeable. This, added to the long uncertainty about remaining in the country, and his increasing anxiety as the time approached when a ship might be expected, had a bad effect on his usually excellent health. Working in the cold warehouse had also left him with a troublesome cough he seemed unable to shake off.

In his diary he complains of feeling 'very feeble and weakened in health and strength compared with former years . . . largely caused by anxiety for the fate of my poor miserable Greenland'. Indeed, so tired and dispirited had he become that when a ship at last arrived from Copenhagen bringing provisions and permission for him to continue with both mission and trade for another year, he seems to have received the news with rather mixed feelings.

'Although I did not receive such pleasurable tidings as I desired about the continuance of the mission', he writes in his diary, 'I have nevertheless every cause to thank the king who has provided us with a ship and provisions for another year . . . thus supporting the mission until further notice so that I am not entirely in despair of a successful issue'. But in a letter to Copenhagen he writes that the ship has brought him 'nothing to lighten his depression' and mentions instructions he has received that if a Danish ship should not arrive next summer he must return in a Dutch one. From this he fears there is little chance of support for the mission once the year he has been granted is over. Only hope and his conscience 'which bade him hold out to the bitter end' now kept him in Greenland.

During the talks in Copenhagen the question of another expedition to the east coast in search of East Bygd was discussed and it was decided to entrust the task to a Norwegian, Mathis Jochimsson, an experienced traveller described as 'lively and outspoken'. He was also instructed to keep a look-out for minerals and metals; for places where cattle might be raised, and the sowing of grain carried out.

This unexpected guest arrived with the supply ship and soon after she returned to Copenhagen went north with a trading expedition that confirmed the sad news of the destruction of Nepisat.

He had not much time before a ship would arrive to take him back to Denmark and immediately after his return to Godthaab he and his men sailed south. They only managed to reach Sermelik fiord, three hundred miles or more short of where Hans had turned back in 1723 !

The fiord itself they found choked with ice after a mile or so, and returning to the open sea again the men, fearful of missing the ship home, were unwilling to continue further south, and reluctantly Jochimsson gave the order to return to Godthaab.

Before leaving for Denmark he tried hard to persuade Hans that the strait marked on the old maps and supposed to lead to the east coast, existed—though probably choked with ice. But Hans only smiled, shook his head, and refused, gently but firmly, to be convinced.

Though Jochimsson had failed, as so many before and after him, to reach the eastern coast, his short stay in Greenland was by no means wasted. He not only wrote an eye-witness's account of the Godthaab settlement at this critical time but a remarkable and whole-hearted appreciation of Hans.

When he arrived, he wrote, he had found both Hans and his wife 'very weak from the cold and a disease of the chest', and continues :

'I have taken the greatest possible pains to find out the reason why the minister and his wife, year after year, keep on doing this work in Greenland and suffering such inconvenience from it,

162

besides having spent everything they possessed in Norway in order to be able to carry it out.

'I admit that at first I thought the minister must have some secret intrigue underlying it all, and wanted to make himself deserving of a bishop's see or a rich living in Denmark or Norway, but I have come to the conclusion that he has no inclination for any such thing and only, as he says, wishes to live and die here in order to teach the savages the knowledge of God'.

And he adds that he also had a suspicion that what made Hans Egede remain in the country might be a wish to make money by sending home goods on his own account or by trading with the Dutch. Daily life at the settlement, however, had convinced him that 'he only tries to work for the honour of God and the benefit of the King, even if it should cost him his life, and that such a man is worth his weight in gold . . .'

And such words can hardly have failed to impress the authorities in Copenhagen; the King, who for religious reasons had now made up his mind to support the mission; and to confirm Severin in his decision and in his faith in Hans.

PART THREE

Unusually early in the spring of 1733 a ship sailed into Godthaab harbour bringing 'glad tidings'. As a result of Hans' 'earnest entreaties' to him, the King had decided to continue to support the missionary work with a substantial yearly sum. The trade was also to receive more attention.

To Hans it was 'glad tidings of great joy'; a definite assurance for the continuing of his work; the long night of uncertainty over, a new day about to break.

But it is said always to be darkest before dawn and he had hardly had time to savour his new happiness before he was plunged into misery and darkness deeper than any he had known before.

On the ship was a young Greenlander who had spent the winter in Denmark. It was obvious that he was a sick man on arrival and very soon evident that the disease from which he was suffering was smallpox.

The safeguard of vaccination lay nearly seventy years in the future; the precaution of isolation still unknown. Travelling northwards to friends he quickly spread the disease.

As often happens in communities cut off, as the Greenlanders were, from much contact with the outside world, even the mildest infection—even the common cold—can cause widespread distress, and often death. Smallpox, one of the most infectious and contagious of all diseases, spread like wildfire among them. By the autumn it had reached the Godthaab district. In spite of Hans' efforts to persuade people to remain in their houses and camps and so lessen the spread of infection, they fled in terror from their sick and dying companions.

Instinctively, like children to their home, those who lived near the settlement sought shelter there; the sick, the distraught, the dying; frightened parents carrying stricken children; frightened children dragging, pushing, stricken parents . . .

Autumn gave place to winter and the disease increased in severity. Whole communities died. In the bitter cold, men, women and children from nearby winter houses huddled together at the settlement doors begging, imploring admission.

As the sailors and most of the settlers, nauseated by the stench and general squalor of the disease, refused them shelter, Hans packed as many as he could into his own quarters, insisting that first all orphaned children, who would otherwise have starved, were admitted.

Daily, in his over-sensitive conscience he blamed himself for the disaster. He, the civilised white man who had set himself to save the souls of a people, had brought about this destruction of their bodies; almost it seemed, the ruin of their race.

It was now that the true character of this steadfast man was seen; the patient love beneath the frequently impatient, often stern, sometimes even harsh manner of his day-to-day living. In a dark hour 'the apostle of Greenland' had been born; in this still darker one the lasting affection and reverence in which he came to be held had its birth. The calm figure with 'the comfortable blue look of hope' in his eyes had become a living expression of the new way of life about which he had been trying to teach them; easier to understand than all his sermons or his books and pictures.

To these stricken men and women it was indeed a new way of life, this Christian way; a way worth imitating.

The words of a dying Greenlander who, when hale and hearty had disdained, even derided, Christianity must have spoken for many.

'You have done for us what not even our own kinsfolk would have done; you have fed us when we were famished; you have buried our dead who would otherwise have been a prey for foxes and ravens. Above all you have told us of God and we may now die happily in hope of a better life hereafter'.

As the cold increased, so did the disease. All other activities put aside Hans gave himself wholly and entirely to the welfare of the sick and dying and homeless. There was no rest by day and all too often little at night, when he had frequently to separate the dead from the living, dragging the bodies into the passage outside for burial in the morning. For a time even the actual burying fell to him after he had found some sailors had robbed a body of its clothes.

Though he must privately have deplored it as pagan, he was often deeply touched by the way in which the Greenlanders, as soon as they felt ill, would make new clothes for themselves, in order to be well and suitably attired in the next world; or sacrifice the family's best reindeer skin to wrap round a dead body.

With the new year the disease made even more rapid progress.

In the Godthaab district it spread with alarming rapidity and Hans had the added distress of learning of the death of the catechist Frederik Christian.

It was a great grief to him shared, as all else at this saddening and tragic time, by the whole Egede family.

No less selfless than that of her husband was the devotion of Fru Egede. Day in, day out, this courageous and indomitable woman nursed, fed and tended the sick and the dying, the old and bereaved, the orphaned and infant children. Though both she and her daughters shrank from the never-ending filth and stench; the continual fear of infection; the discouragement of so many and frequent deaths, and the close confinement in such cramped and crowded quarters, they questioned nothing. These were their people; men, women and children to be saved, helped and comforted.

Kirsten and Petronella were young and strong. Though they worked hard by day, at night they slept the deep unbroken sleep of youth, oblivious of the anguish around them, and their mother saw to it they were not disturbed. But she herself had no such respite. Continually broken nights followed the incessant toil by day. Only a woman of remarkable constitution could have survived the stresses and strains, the anxieties and responsibilities and the hard physical work that had been hers almost from the hour of her marriage. Now she was no longer young. The outbreaks of illness in 1728-29 that had left practically no one untouched; the recent hard and heavy work in the cold, unheated warehouse, added to the constant uncertainty of the last two years, had all helped to undermine her health. Throughout the whole nine months of the epidemic with quiet courage she worked through each difficult day; but as Hans was to write later, 'After that time my beloved wife suffered greatly in loss of strength and health, nay, from that day she was never well, until God in his mercy called her to Him'.

It was not until the late spring that the disease finally spent itself. Nearly all those in the neighbourhood of the settlement were dead. To the south, and as far as eighty miles northwards, entire communities had died. Scattered everywhere unburied bodies began to be visible under the now melting snow.

Out of a population of about 12,000 Hans estimated that between two and three thousand must have died.

In the spring of 1734 the merchant Jacob Severin sent three ships to Greenland. The first to arrive brought the news that he had taken over both the trade and the mission, and, among other things, was arranging to establish a settlement in the whaling area around Disko Bay, not far from Nepisat.

Exhausted in body and mind from his recent exertions, Hans was 'lifted up' as he describes it in his diary, by the news, and though he had some misgivings which he expressed later, for the time being these were overshadowed by other news he received. Paul was on his way home! He was on board a second ship sailing direct to Disko Bay and was to come south with it later in the summer.

Paul on his way! In an agony of impatience Hans waited while the Captain, a slow, deliberate man, handed over letters and official documents and papers, and finally plunged heavily into an account of his voyage. At last he could bear it no longer; begging the Captain to excuse him he tore himself away and hurrying back to the settlement burst in with the news.

Fru Egede, as so often happened now, was resting on her bed, Kirsten reading aloud to her.

Paul on his way . . . she could hardly believe it! It was six years all but two months since she had seen him . . . six years!

166

When he left she had thought she could never endure the three, possibly four, he might be away; the dreadful fear that something might happen; that she might never see him again. How often during these last terrible months she had experienced that fear again; prayed that she might live until his return!

Hope gave her strength. The next day she was up and busying herself with hospitality to the garrulous captain and those with him before they sailed north.

Paul too was longing to be with his family again. Though he had been happy in Denmark, because of the unsettled state of affairs in Greenland his studies had had to be carried on in a disturbing atmosphere of uncertainty and at one time it looked very doubtful if he would ever be able to take up missionary work there.

For a while it almost seemed as if his boyhood dream of being a naval officer might yet come true—he had even received a promise from King Frederik to accept him as a midshipman. But once the new king had finally agreed to support both the trade and the missionary work there was no choice; the dream faded away, this time for good, and Paul settled down to concentrate on his studies for the priesthood.

Early in 1734 he took the degree of Bachelor of Divinity, and shortly after was ordained by the Bishop of Copenhagen.

Before leaving for Greenland he was received in audience by King Christian, who congratulated him on his success, and promised him a suitable living whenever he might return.

It was only after he boarded the ship which, together with two other missionaries, was to take him to Greenland, that Paul learnt the Captain had orders not to call at Godthaab but to sail direct to Disko Bay.

It was a great disappointment but the wonderful welcome he received from Greenlanders camping round about helped to make up for it. Many who had once lived in or near Godthaab and grown up with him, received him with joy, proudly pointing out to their friends how he spoke to them in their own language. Others who had never met him, but had heard him much praised and spoken about, crowded round begging him to stay among them. But Paul shook his head, explaining that he had first to build a house and then go south to his parents for a time. Later, he would return to them, for good.

167

This time timber had been brought from Denmark in ready-sawn planks and the settlement house was quickly built. On June 25th Paul preached his first sermon there and gave the name of Christianshaab to the new colony. Late in July he left by ship for Godthaab.

If ever there was a joyous homecoming this was one! But for all her quiet happiness; her pride, when Paul, on his first Sunday with them, appeared in all the glory of gown, ruff, and wig, to assist his father at the settlement service, it was plain to everyone that Fru Egede was growing weaker.

Ships arriving in Copenhagen in the autumn of 1734 brought good news concerning the founding of Christianshaab. They also brought the first reports of the smallpox epidemic and its terrible toll of life; while their holds, almost empty of cargo, spoke more eloquently than any documents of its effect on the trade.

Glad as Hans had been to learn that Severin had taken over both trade and missionary work, he had doubts about some of his proposed schemes and these he expressed in a report sent back by one of the ships.

'Unless God bless the new undertaking in Disko Bay', he wrote, he was doubtful of its success, for no help could be expected from Godthaab, now 'practically a desert . . . the best of the trading posts exterminated'.

In the depression that was beginning to beset him and which even the joy of Paul's return had not entirely been able to dispel, now for the first time he expresses a definite wish to leave Greenland. He is 'weary', he writes, 'of all these fatalities', and of the little he considers has been achieved 'both from a spiritual and from a temporal point of view'.

It says much for Severin's faith and tenacity of purpose that he remained undaunted by all these setbacks and gloomy forebodings. In spite of great difficulties he was to continue the work he had undertaken for sixteen years, determined Hans Egede's work should not be undone, and believing, like him, that the missionary and colonising work were one.

He soon realised that the presence, at least, of armed force would be necessary to restrain the Dutch from interfering with the trade, and petitioned the King for a frigate to be sent up early each year, and a stern warning issued to the Dutch Government.

A few skirmishes took place over the years but gradually Danish sovereignty came to be respected, order established, trade unmolested.

A great deal is owed to Jacob Severin. To his courage and enterprise; his firmness in adversity and his faith in Greenland's future. Before he left the country he had extended colonisation as far as 72° North; appointed four missionaries, and established schools at Godthaab and Christianshaab.

In the words inscribed on the monument to him in his native town, 'He came to the rescue of Hans Egede and he preserved Greenland for Denmark.'

During the long winter Fru Egede scarcely left her bed and though when the spring came again and during the summer she was sometimes able to sit up in a chair for a short time it was obviously only by an immense effort of will. By August, when Hans, who had now received permission to leave Greenland, had hoped to take her back to Denmark he felt he dared not risk the hardships of the long voyage for her. In the autumn she seemed better for a time and he allowed himself to leave the settlement for short periods, but late in November, returning from a visit to some Greenlanders living near he found her so weak he realised there was no hope of her recovery. On December 21st she died.

'Throughout two centuries', writes the Danish historian Louis Bobé, 'the memory of this unusual woman has been honoured in the wild country to which she gave her soul'.

In the still partly wild but civilised Greenland of today the name of Gertrud Egede is held in almost as much reverence and affection as that of her husband, 'her Abraham' as he had once written of himself in their Lofoten days; a thought he repeats in the tender memorial, too long to quote in full, which he wrote of her. His 'dear and faithful helpmate and wife . . . who when she understood that I had resolved . . . to forsake my native country . . . even though relations and friends violently opposed it and implored her for the sake of her own welfare, for mine, and for that of our small children not to consent to so rash and foolhardy an enterprise, yet for love of God and me, like a faithful Sara . . . accompanied her Abraham to a strange, nay, hard and heathen country . . .'

Unable to bear the thought of leaving her body in Greenland

he had a coffin specially constructed so that he might take her with him for 'a seemly and Christian burial in Denmark'.

The year was nearly over. On New Year's Eve, among other entries in his diary, Hans wrote, 'Thus the old year ended . . . sadly enough for me but for her . . . in bliss and joy'.

It was exactly a month before his forty-ninth birthday.

Strong as he was, Hans too had been overstrained by the long drawn-out epidemic. For the first time in his life he was suffering from scurvy, often a very depressing disease, and once again from a troublesome cough. With the death of his wife it seemed as if some powerful inner strength had left him; his tired spirit spent. Entries in his diary show that he was sometimes seized with fits of melancholy, deep and terrifying; a black depression which no prayer seemed able to overcome. An acute shortage of vital foods due to their having been used for the smallpox victims may well have been responsible for much of this. Whatever the cause, and in spite of a fine, mild spring, he remained weak and strengthless, unable even to preach at the settlement services.

Meanwhile the news of his coming departure had spread far and wide. At the end of April five umiaks arrived at Godthaab filled with Greenlanders from the north who had come to spend a little time with him before he left and receive his last instructions to them A few days later they were joined by others, and throughout the next few weeks umiaks and kayaks were continually arriving and departing.

By Whit Sunday he had recovered sufficiently to preach at the settlement, and at the end of May, though still weak, he insisted on making one last journey. It was to the district around Nepisat where so many Greenlanders gathered for their summer fishing and hunting.

It was a brief visit, sad with the sadness of farewell, but the obvious distress at the sight of his now worn and bent figure and the joyful welcome he was given can have left him in no doubt of the affection in which he was held by these people.

But in spite of this he wondered, in the depression that still beset him, how much of his teaching had taken root? How long they would remember? Then he reminded himself that Paul would be there, and later Niels, who was to return after a short stay in Denmark.

170

He was indeed fortunate in his sons, he reflected; both so beloved by the Greenlanders; both so devoted to them. Only the hand on the plough would be changed, and—the ghost of a smile flickered over his sad face—it would still be an Egede hand!

As his men rowed him homewards he sat thinking of many things; seeing for the last time the lovely line of coast, the icy barren mountains, the stretches of fertile land, vivid now in summer greenness, gay with patches of poppies and bog-cotton; listening to the cries and mewings of sea-birds and the cheepings of the fleets of newly-hatched little eider ducks. Eider ducks . . . how Gertrud had loved them! . . . . The Lord had given—and taken away. . . . But—the earth was still His, and the fullness thereof. . . .

Not long after the return to Godthaab the supply ship arrived. And literally not a day too soon. Those at the settlement were on the verge of starvation; even the hunting had been poor. Apart from small supplies of fish and game the only food left was exactly one and a half barrels of grain.

On June 21st, Paul said a sad goodbye to his family and went north with the ship.

On June 29th Hans preached his farewell sermon at the settlement, taking as his text the melancholy words of Isaiah so sadly in keeping with his feelings of depression.

'I said I have laboured in vain; I have spent my strength for naught and in vain, yet surely my judgement is with the Lord and my work with my God'.

Speaking with much of his old vigour he refers to what he considers the poor results of his work, and also his belief that, with his failing health, he will better serve them all by returning to Denmark and directing the missionary work from there than by attempting to remain in Greenland.

'For', as he ends, with words that are at the same time impassioned yet gentle, 'as I came here, not for temporal benefit and gain, in the like manner I do not leave Greenland for temporal benefit and gain; only the honour of God and the teaching of a poor and ignorant people has been, and always will be, my one and only aim, nay, the eternal wish of my heart until my death'.*

The few remaining weeks were taken up with packing, matters concerning the trade and some final instructions by Hans to

* Recorded in Diary of July 29th, 1736.

those living close to the settlement. Almost his last act before leaving the country was to baptise a young Greenland boy he had been instructing for the last two years, giving him his own name, Hans.

On August 9th, together with Niels, Kirsten and Petronella, he sailed from Godthaab for Copenhagen. Carried in the same ship in the coffin he had had specially constructed, was the body of his beloved Gertrud.

In the early evening of August 21st the ship neared Cape Farewell. Standing on the deck for a last glimpse of Greenland, Hans saw the magnificent chain of mountains that form the coast line there, so frequently shrouded in cloud or fog, revealed in all their glory. In the glow of evening they stood, serene and shining, a last salute from the country he had served with devotion for fifteen years, and to which he had given his soul for ever.

13

From Greenland's Icy Mountains

PART ONE

On September 24th, 1736, Hans and his family arrived in Copenhagen after what he describes as 'a rather long and arduous voyage'. Actually, approaching the coast of Norway in dense fog combined with a south-westerly gale they were in grave danger. The ship was being driven towards the cliffs and would undoubtedly have been wrecked had the wind not suddenly veered to the north-west, 'and thus, by the mercy of God, we escaped this great danger'.

Long and arduous or not, Hans had benefitted greatly from the voyage. He was always a good sailor and with adequate food and, for the first time for many years, freedom from worry of one kind or another, his strong body and resilient spirit re-asserted themselves. The tired and melancholy man who had written the last Greenland diaries was gone. Nor, unlike his children, particularly the outdoor-loving Niels, did he find it hard after living so long in isolated and primitive conditions to adapt himself to the busy life of Copenhagen.

Having reported his arrival to the Missionary College he remained quietly at the city house of Jacob Severin until after the funeral of his wife. This took place at the Nicolai Church and besides the family and many friends, was attended by the clergy of the city, professors of divinity from the University, and by the Bishop of Zeeland, the island on which Copenhagen is built.

Three days later, on the instructions of the Missionary College, he journeyed to Fredensborg for an audience with the King.

Apart from what he had heard publicly and been told privately, Christian VI was anxious to meet this adventurous clergyman-subject of his. Like his father, the new King was impressed with Hans' sincerity and single-mindedness; his strange mixture of simplicity and shrewdness, so often the mark of great men, appealed to him. Hans gave him a full account of the mission-

173

ary work, and during the three days he remained in Fredensborg, he and the King met several times, talking together as man to man rather than across the gulf then separating subject from monarch.

Encouraged and heartened, full of plans for the future Hans returned to Copenhagen, found a lodging for himself and his family, and with all his old zest plunged headlong into the writing of reports and into schemes and proposals for the future. By the end of October he had sent to both the King and the Missionary College detailed accounts of his work in Greenland from the day he landed until the day he left with many suggestions for the future.

Among other matters he particularly stressed the need for all who wished to be missionaries in Greenland to spend one to two years in learning the language before going there, offering for a small salary to teach it. He also suggested the training of boys from the Royal Orphanage as catechists and assistant Traders. In this too he was prepared to assist if accommodation for himself and his family could be provided at the Orphanage.

The need for some kind of paid work was daily becoming more urgent for him. His salary, promised him as a pension, had not been paid since his arrival in Denmark and in any case, as he had soon realised, would never be sufficient to support himself and his family in a city like Copenhagen. Moreover in Greenland he had received free lodging, cramped and uncomfortable as it was, fuel, and necessary stores. It had even been possible to save money and on these savings he was now living. But they were rapidly dwindling.

Unlike Greenland—unlike even Lofoten—life in Copenhagen seemed to demand so many unnecessary things. His daughters, at first bewildered by the city's shops and markets, were soon asking for clothes and adornments like other girls they met.

Gone were the days when he in a worn black gown rapidly turning green with age, and Niels in hooded sealskin coat and trousers, need take no thought for the morrow of what they should put on or wherewithal they should be clothed!

In Copenhagen both today and tomorrow it was necessary to wear clean, tidy garments. For himself a new black gown in which to preach; for Niels a suit of stout woollen cloth, even a hat. Niels detested them both! He would wander down to the

174

quays and stand staring moodily seawards, aching with home-sickness; for comfortable seal-skin, for ice-floes, and for dark, flat-nosed faces ...

At the end of three months the Missionary College, so frequently unresponsive and slow to move, was apparently still pondering their copy of Hans' report when they received a letter from the King. The warm interest Hans had aroused in him had found practical expression, and in the letter he announced his intention of founding two Seminaries, one where students could be trained for missionary work in Greenland; the other for boys from the Royal Orphanage who, when older, would be willing to serve as catechists or Assistant traders.

Hans was delighted when the news reached him. For any of his ideas to be approved without long arguments, letters, and waiting was a new—and exhilarating experience. But one thing troubled him. The problem of earning a living was still unsolved; his pension still unpaid. Not only were all his savings spent but he was now in debt to friends for necessary food and clothing.

Reluctantly, and with distaste, more certain than ever that while the love of money was the root of all evil, the day to day need for it was all too closely related, he shut himself in his room and wrote a letter to the King.

As shortly and plainly as possible he explained his position. The impossibility of keeping himself and his family on his promised pension; the stark fact that since his arrival in Denmark no payment had been made to him so that now, his savings all spent, he was in debt—owing 300 Rigsdaler to friends for food and clothing ...

A fair-minded, if unimaginative man, King Christian lost no time in seeing the promised pension was paid, and from the day of arrival. A yearly sum of two hundred Rigsdaler (then worth about £40) was also to be added to it, though this, it was frankly stated, was to encourage future missionaries to Greenland. And the debt to friends would be paid 'by special grace'.

For the next two and a half years or so all Hans' time seems to have been taken up with writing; pamphlets, translations, aids to learning Greenlandic and finally, the first of his two best-known books—an account of the Greenland mission; the exploring of the country, and the ways of the inhabitants.

For both book and pamphlets he used the careful, detailed,

day to day diaries he had never failed to keep, one for each of the fifteen years he had spent in Greenland, wisely adding little to them.

Written in scanty leisure moments and enforced periods of idleness; huddled over the stove while the blizzards raged on long mid-winter nights; risking frost-bitten fingers lying under an up-turned boat; seldom in comfort, rarely free from distractions, these diaries were, alas, all lost in the great fire of Copenhagen in 1795. Fortunately most of the pamphlets, the book and its successor which he wrote later, remain.

In spite of the harsh conditions under which they were written, perhaps even because of them, the short, terse, diary sentences reveal far more than they actually say; the dangers and discomforts, the disappointments, the unending toil. Here and there one catches a glimpse of Hans himself; his faults and failings, his courage, and the courage of those who had worked with him. Above all, the immensity of the task he had set himself.

Meanwhile the building of the Greenland Seminary promised by the King had been going ahead; early in 1740 it was completed. There can have been little doubt as to who was best qualified to be in charge of it, and no one, except perhaps Hans himself, was surprised when he was appointed its first Superintendent.

From now the whole pattern of his life was changed. He was responsible for much of the Greenland mission; the training of missionaries and catechists, and the teaching of Greenlandic.

A quiet joy possessed him; a deep thankfulness; a certainty that work for Greenland, whether in his hands or another's would go on. 'The hungry sheep look up'—be fed. . . .

He lost no time in setting about his duties at the Institute and was happily engrossed in them when he received an unexpected letter from Paul. For some time he wrote, his health had not been good; his eyes particularly, had been troubling him; now his sight had become so bad that he must return to Denmark and would arrive in the autumn.

Paul's departure was a great loss to Greenland, particularly Christianshaab, the colony he had founded.

'There is nothing the matter with thy mouth', the Greenlanders there protested when he explained his reason for returning to Denmark, 'so do not speak of leaving us.'

Throughout the whole Disko Bay area where many now lived who had known him as a child, and where he was greatly loved, there was distress at the news. It was these Greenlanders who, when he had built his house with its proud white flagstaff on his arrival in 1734, had paid him one of their greatest compliments. His 'floor', they assured him 'would never be free of their feet'—a statement to which they were to remain almost embarrassingly faithful!

Today that same house, filled so often with the pad and shuffle of fur-clad feet, still stands, the Christianshaab offices of the Royal Greenland Trade. The mountains remain unchanged; the small bergs still drift in the harbour, but today the fur-clad feet are mostly shod in rubber or in leather; and in place of quietly moving kayaks, motor-boats chug noisily among the floes. In the little town there is a church and school; a big shrimp cannery, and modern shops. But the name of Paul Egede, 'Pavia' as he was called, is still held in loving memory and descendents of the many he baptised, among them those of his first girl-converts christened Kirsten and Petronella after his two sisters, both play their part, in today's happy, well-governed, and Christian Greenland.

Meanwhile Greenland's loss was Hans' gain, though in the end perhaps Greenland's too.

Paul arrived in Copenhagen in the late autumn and shortly after was appointed chaplain at Vartov, then an Institution for homeless children.

It was a condition of the appointment that any spare time should be devoted to translation work, and to assisting with the teaching at the new Seminary.

Somehow, during his busy years at Christianshaab, Paul had found time to translate two of the gospels and the first three books of the Old Testament. Now, with the Egede zeal for work, and in spite of poor health and failing eyesight, he entered on his new duties with zest.

By 1744 all four gospels were ready for publication; the first translation of the Bible into Greenlandic. They were followed in the years ahead by the long Lutheran catechism, and finally by the complete New Testament.

From the earliest days of his arrival in Greenland, Hans had been making notes for a Greenlandic grammar but, unlike Paul, he had never been able to learn the language well enough to make a satisfactory book. Now between them it was completed, while Hans in his turn, with his greater knowledge of Latin, helped Paul in his struggles with a Greenlandic-Danish-Latin dictionary on which he had embarked. This very difficult work they also finished between them, and both books were used in the Seminary.

But perhaps what they enjoyed most was the preparing of Hans' second and best-known book 'Det Nye Grønlands Perlustration'— 'A New Description of Greenland'.

As together they read through his closely written, stained and dog-eared diaries, his notes and reports, how many shared experiences must have been remembered!

Sometimes, with this and the work on the dictionary, for brief moments it almost seemed to Hans that they were back in Greenland, sitting round the table on a dark winter's day with the lesson books open . . . his voice raised against the blizzard screaming past the windows, or in impatience with Niels, reluctant and rebellious, or with Petronella weeping over her reading. . . . And he would glance at Paul holding a book close to his eyes, wrestling with some untranslatable Greenlandic word, and wonder sadly whether his son's sight would have fared better had he served his country, as he had once wished, as a sailor, instead of among the Greenland snows. . . . Then his thoughts would stray to Niels —Niels who had always known what he wanted, and usually done it, and yet been led—and how unexpectedly—to bring light into dark places! . . . And Kirsten, and the once tearful Petronella, long since grown-up, now both engaged to be married. Sometimes it seemed to him like yesterday; sometimes all, or more, of the twenty years it really was. . . .

The book was quickly written. Hans had already planned and made notes for it in Greenland. All he needed were his diaries and copies of reports he had sent back over the years to Denmark.

It was a great success. Even today, apart from its interest as history, it has a strange charm. At the time it was written it was different from anything of its kind.

'From its first appearance', writes Louis Bobé, 'it attracted great attention and was translated into several languages . . . with this description of a hitherto little known country . . . its geography, its climate and fauna . . . the name of Hans Egede became famous all over Europe . . . all that father and son had been able to learn about the Greenlanders . . . is here set forth'.

In England there were several editions; in 1818 one with illustrations, two of which are reproduced in this book, that were probably based on Paul's drawings.

Both this book and Hans' earlier one were printed by the Royal Orphanage but only on condition he received no profit for himself until the sales had paid for the cost of printing them. As a result, although the books sold well, and still continue to sell, they can have brought him little money during his lifetime. But he was content. Not that his name was 'famous all over Europe' but because Greenland, her people, and her needs would now be more widely known.

PART TWO

Like a ship that has reached harbour after a long and storm-tossed voyage, for the next few years Hans was at peace. He had work that he loved, in close companionship with Paul. The pleasure of seeing both his daughters happily married to men, who, though by no means prosperous by this world's standards, had all the qualities he admired, Kirsten to Lauritz Alsbach who had been for a time a missionary in Greenland; Petronella to Jørgens Saabye, then in charge of the small island parish of Strynø, near Fyn. Both young men were to become very dear to him.

It was also during this time that he received the offer of the Bishopric of Trondheim. It was a tremendous honour, perhaps the greatest that could have been bestowed on a still poor, if not by now unknown clergyman, with no high academic attainments. But touched and grateful as he was; regretful that his Gertrud had not lived to share such happy news, and sensitive to the disappointment he knew his decision would be to his old parishioners in Lofoten, Hans had no hesitation in refusing. Such honours were not for him. As he had said in his farewell sermon at Godthaab, Greenland and the welfare of her people were, and always would be, the chief concern of his life.

It was not possible such peace could continue indefinitely. As time went on Hans frequently found himself in disagreement with the Missionary College, especially about the way the Godthaab settlement was being managed. In 1747 he resigned.

179

The following year he left Copenhagen for good.

Paul succeeded him as Superintendent at the Seminary, and not long after was appointed Professor of Divinity in the University, and later Honorary Bishop of Greenland. He continued with his teaching and translating work until his eyesight failed completely and forced him to retire. Even when quite blind he continued to work for Greenland, and his love for the country and its people remained with him to the end of his long life.

Today the name of Paul Egede is honoured throughout the country and every schoolchild there knows the story of the boy who had once wished to be a sailor but became instead a great missionary.

In 1740, when the original charter granted to Jacob Severin for the navigation of Greenland and the upkeep of the mission was renewed, he appointed Niels, then back at Godthaab, to be chief Trader at Christianshaab.

It was a wise decision. Niels Egede, 'Nise' as they called him, was a man the Greenlanders could trust and respect. Besides being strong and sturdy in body they knew him to be kindly and sympathetic, familiar with their language, and happy in their companionship.

Both as trader and as missionary Niels was tireless. He quickly improved the trade, and very soon established two little missionary stations, naming the larger one Jacobshaven in honour of Severin. Any time left over from his trading duties he devoted entirely to the Greenlanders, joining in their games or singing with them; teaching or preaching to them; and sometimes, like his father before him, resorting to 'a little chastisement' if they failed to pay due attention to his words!

In 1743, for some reason now unknown, Niels returned from Greenland to a Government appointment at Aalborg in northeastern Denmark; and here, the year after he left the Institute, Hans went to stay with him.

'He will do well, you will see', Fru Egede had once said of Niels. Many times down the years the calm certainty of his wife's words had come back to Hans; but how well he was not to live to see . . .

While they were together at Aalborg father and son became very close to each other and after Hans' death, when Niels returned to Greenland entrusted with the building of a new settlement north of Christianshaab, he named it Egedesminde (Egedes-town)—after his father.

For many years Niels continued to work in Greenland returning occasionally to Denmark for a short stay.

On one of these visits, in recognition of his work, he was presented by Prince—later King, Frederik VI—with a watch, gold and set with brilliants; a valued and valuable gift, if a little unsuitable for wearing in Greenland!

As the years went by there were few Greenlanders who had not heard of Nise the Trader; Nise The Preacher, or 'Speaker of Words'. Before he finally left their country he was known and loved throughout the whole of south-west Greenland, even north of Disko Bay.

Today 'Nise' Egede, like Paul, is remembered and honoured; for his colonising ability; for his devotion to his work; above all, for his love of the Greenlanders.

In 1781, then over seventy years of age, he returned to Denmark for good.

He had spent nearly fifty years in the service of the country to which he had come as a young boy; he had been awarded a high Danish honour, the King's medal 'pro meritas'; Fru Egede's words had come true!

After some time at Aalborg, Hans went to stay with Kirsten and her husband, then rector of Vardal, a little township about 80 miles from Christiania and not far from Lake Mjösa in southeast Norway.

It was nearly thirty years, he reflected as he sailed up the Kattegat, since he had set foot on Norwegian soil!

As he journeyed to Vardal he thought how different a countryside this was from his birth-place in Hinnöy with its rocks and boulders, its waterfalls and rushing rivers; or his home among the jagged peaks of Lofoten with the sea pounding the rocks in winter or softly lapping in the long light summer. Here the mountains were low; in the wide valleys cornfields and rich grazing-land, prosperous farms and placidly flowing rivers. And though his heart ached a little for a sight of his home across the Circle, it was all Norway; his own country. He had come home.

If Kirsten and her husband had remained at Vardal; if Paul, Niels and Petronella were not all living in Denmark, Hans might still have journeyed north; visited Harstad and the vicarage at Kabelvåg; seen Vågekallen once more; stood again on a certain little sandy beach. . . .

But it was not to be. Unexpectedly his son-in-law was appointed rector of Stubbekøbing in Falster, a small island in the Baltic some way south of Copenhagen. As the Rectory was large, too large for the needs of only Kirsten and her husband they persuaded Hans to go with them; to make it his home too. And in the peace of this small Baltic island he lived, in quiet happiness, for the few remaining years of his life.

Chemistry still remained one of Hans' many interests. Now with plenty of space and leisure he was able to spend many happy hours conducting experiments; pouring liquids into test tubes; pounding away with a pestle and mortar, and peering down a microscope. A friend meeting him in the spring of 1757, some eighteen months before he died, found him 'gay, pleasant, and, as a result of his plain living in perfect health'. His eyesight too, remained excellent. Another friend describes him as 'pleased in God, charitable to the poor as far as his modest means allowed, and loved and honoured for his quiet ways'.

But it was always Greenland and the work there that remained nearest to his heart.

Sometimes in summer, sitting in the rectory garden, his blue eyes, faded a little now, had a far away look in them as if beyond the smooth boles of the beech trees, his daughter's carefully tended flower beds, and the gently lapping waters of the Baltic he saw another landscape . . . Greenland in summer . . . icy mountains and lush green grass, white and yellow poppies swaying in the wind; wheeling sea-birds and leaping fish; fleets of little eider-ducks . . . but perhaps most plainly, small fur-clad figures gathering at a summer camp. . . . And the wind blowing in from the great ocean to the west and rustling softly in the garden trees seemed to bring a sound that only he could hear . . . a sound like singing; faint and far away; like an evening hymn heard in the distance at sunset . . .

Hans was growing old now. Nearly fifty years had passed since that October evening when, a young man, he stood on the beach at Kabelvåg and heard a Voice speak so plainly to him. Nearly fifty years of unbroken devotion to a cause.

Early in November 1758, a little over two months before his 73rd birthday, he died.

'Explorer; coloniser; missionary'; Hans Egede was all three. He did not, as some have wrongly believed, discover Greenland. He re-discovered it. He was an explorer, a 'land-taker' to use the old Norse term, of lasting and far-reaching importance.

'The first settler in Greenland' since the days of the Norsemen writes Louis Bobé, 'he alone struck root in the wild and barren country where all before him had only been birds of passage. His miserable dwelling on Hope Island became a stronghold of Christianity and the centre of colonisation along an inhospitable coast. Had he not stood firm in the critical year of 1730 Greenland would probably have been lost to Denmark. . . . His work and that of his devoted wife remains one of the brightest chapters in the history of the Protestant Church.'

But perhaps Hans was never more fittingly described than in the words chosen as text by the preacher at his funeral.

'There was a man sent from God whose name was John.* The same came . . . to bear witness of the Light that all men through him might believe . . .'

The funeral service was held at Stubbekøbing, but Hans was buried as he had wished, beside his wife in Copenhagen.

Engraved on his tombstone, after his name, was this brief inscription :

'An honour among Christians;
A light to heathens.
Famous in Norway,
Revered in Denmark
But in Greenland, immortal.'

A great tribute to a great man.

* 'Hans' is an abbreviation of Johannes—Danish (and Norwegian) for John.

14
Greenland Today

It is now over two hundred years since the death of Hans Egede; but what of the country that he served, the once remote and long neglected land; the long-lost colony reclaimed by him for Christianty and for civilisation?

Until quite recent years Greenland seems to have been regarded by too many countries as a barely habitable and rather useless polar land; an unenviable—and unenvied—Danish outpost; to some little more than the birthplace of bad weather; the home of the 'cold front' and the 'deep depression'. Today it is slowly being realised that here is a country of great interest, opportunity and increasing importance.

No country can have changed so rapidly since the beginning of this century. Then, in all but the larger settlements, except for church, school and some personal possessions such as fire-arms, tobacco, some modern clothing and cooking utensils, many Greenlanders still lived much as when Hans Egede came among them; as their ancestors had lived for a thousand years or more; stoneage men, entirely dependent on hunting.

Almost overnight as time is reckoned their way of life was changed. Before the first quarter of the century was over, the outboard motor, the flying boat and the aeroplane; electricity, the telephone and telegraph, and a little later wireless, had all reached Greenland. Stone age man was rubbing shoulders with twentieth century man; the primitive hunter with the modern technician.

Today, in most of the larger and many of the smaller settlements, besides churches and schools, there are libraries and hospitals and shops. There are mines and modern canneries. The icy mountains echo to the clang of hammers and the whine of electric drills, and power stations, harbours and roads are being built or improved. In the north and east polar bears and foxes, seal and walrus are still hunted. All through the year, often in temperatures many degrees below zero, the men manning the lonely weather stations in the east send out their wireless reports;

and in the sheltered valleys of the south-west, where Erik's flocks and herds once fed, crops are sown and cattle graze again.

But of the many changes in this land of change one of the most surprising is that at Søndre Strømfiord. Here, where less than thirty years ago, except for rare and distant thunder, nothing louder than the cries of sea-birds and the baying of dogs had been heard, stands a most important air port. A pivot of jet air traffic; the shortest route linking Denmark with Greenland, and a re-fuelling base for the 'Polar Route' flights from Copenhagen to Los Angeles and the Far East.

Stone age and jet age have met. The old has not yet dis-appeared; the new not fully come. The great unpeopled soli-tudes remain; the countless fiords; the rarely visited fells; myriads of skerries and small islands, mile upon mile of sparsely popu-lated coast.

Such, very briefly, is Greenland today. What will be the future of this developing but by no means fully developed country; this land of infinite promise and opportunity?

With increasing prosperity the problem of nearly every nation is fast becoming Greenland's too; the problem of man himself:

'Where shall wisdom be found, and where is the place of un-derstanding?'

The questions asked by Job echo round the world. Will Green-land keep her simplicity; her 'ancient wisdom and austere con-trol', or will she, too, be caught up in today's greedy clamour?

'The ceaseless turmoil of cities', wrote the explorer Nansen, 'the nightmare of money-making is dwarfing the race. . . . There must be a new era with new ideals . . . every spiritual discovery, every conquest in the world of spirit . . . be greeted with the enthusiasm now accorded to material progress.' And, 'It is from the deserts, from the solitudes the new men have always come'.

Perhaps in Greenland's great solitudes this new and more kindly civilisation will be born; the words of the old hymn be reversed; the call to, not from, Greenland's Icy Mountains go forth.

Meanwhile on a low headland overlooking Godthaab stands a figure in gown and ruff, holding a staff, 'The Apostle of Greenland', Hans Egede, still watching over his flock.

ARCTIC OCEAN

○ NORD

GREENLAND SEA

CANADA

THULE

Baffin Bay

Clavering Island

INLAND ICE

UPERNAVIK

Disko Island

UMANAK

Scoresby Sound

QUTDLIGSSAT

GODHAVN

JAKOBSHAVN

EGEDESMINDE

CHRISTIANSHAAB

HOLSTEINSBORG

Søndre Strømfiord

Arctic Circle

SUKKERTOPPEN

ANGMAGSSALIK

ICELAND

GODTHAAB

Amerilik Fiord

FAERINGEHAVN

Denmark Strait

SKJOLDUNGEN

FREDERIKSHAAB

GRONNEDAL

NARSARSSUAQ

IVIGTUT

NARSSAQ

IGALIKO

JULIANEHAAB

NANORTALIK

Cape Farewell

0 100 200 300 400 500 km.

NORTH ATLANTIC

Nepisat was close to present Holsteinsborg

H.J.B

1. Greenland, showing principal settlements at the time of the Royal Tour, 1952. The Davis Strait is off the west coast.

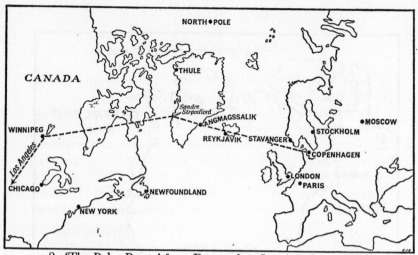

2. 'The Polar Route' from Denmark to Los Angeles and the Far East.

3. Greenland has an area of 840,000 square miles, and with the exception of Australia, is the world's largest island. The distance from north to south is approximately 1,600 miles, and a good idea of the country's size can be gained from these two maps.

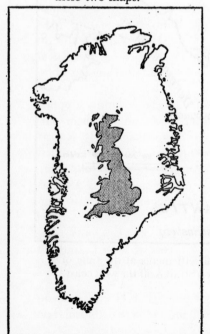

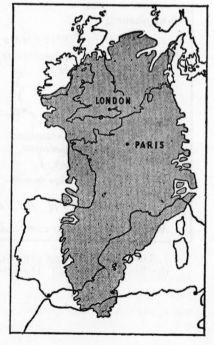

ACKNOWLEDGEMENTS

For permission to include photographs, prints, maps etc. my grateful thanks are due to the following :

Professor Axel Revold of Lysaker, Oslo, for the photograph of his altarpiece in Harstad church; Dr Hans Egede Glahn of Hellerup, Copenhagen, for the photograph of the silver tankard presented to Hans Egede; Hr. fhv. Overnotar Harald Lindow, and Messrs. Rosenkilde & Bagger for the print of the ruins of Hvalsö Church; The Very Reverend K. Nissen, formerly Dean of Tromsö, for two maps from his contribution 'Hans Egede as Geographer and Cartographer' in Hans Egede 1686-1758 published by the Egede Instituttet; The Reverend H. C. Mamen of Oslo, for the photograph of Hans Egede from his contribution, 'Hans Egede as seen by artists' in Hans Egede 1686-1758 published by The Egede Instituttet; Magister Christian Vibe and Det Schønbergske Forlag, Copenhagen, for the photograph 'Confirmation Candidates'; Civilingeniør Mogens Lindhard and Det Schønbergske Forlag, Copenhagen, for the photograph of Godthaab. The Directorate of Posts and Telegraphs, Copenhagen, for the Hans Egede anniversary stamp; Miss Linda Thü for the photograph of the Hans Egede statue in Oslo; The Press and Information Department of the Royal Danish Ministry for Foreign Affairs, for all other photographs.

My grateful thanks are also due to all who have so kindly supplied information and helped me in various ways, among them, Hr. Poul Balle, The Royal Danish Library, Copenhagen; Hr. Robert Petersen, The Nationalmuseet, Copenhagen; Hr. Bent Gynther, The Ministry for Greenland, Copenhagen; Lt. Col. John Thü, The Royal Norwegian Army; Hr. Bengt Petersen, Press Attaché, Royal Danish Embassy, Oslo; Fru Sofie Wigum, Librarian, University of Bergen; Mr. David Howarth, author of *The Shetland Bus* etc; Mr. Geoffrey Wiliamson, author of *Changing Greenland*; my cousin Lt.-Com. C. J. de C. Scott, R.N.retd.; and not least, my niece Mrs. Peggy Molloy for typing the ms from my almost unreadable writing.

Especially I wish to thank Dr. Nils Egede Bloch-Hoell for devoting so much time and patience to giving me verbal information and for reading and advising on the ms; and Miss Lettice Loughnan, formerly English mistress at Selwyn House School, Christchurch, New Zealand, without whose encouragement and practical help the book would never have been completed.

Eve Garnett

The four lines from G. K. Chesterton's poem *The Ballad of the White Horse* are reproduced by kind permission of Miss D. E. Collins and Methuen & Co Ltd.

The One End Street Stories

Written and Illustrated by
EVE GARNETT

Further Adventures of the Family from One End Street

'No one else writes like Eve Garnett. Her gentle, detailed stories, matched exactly by her drawings, will satisfy readers over and over again.'
—*Junior Bookshelf*

Holiday at the Dew Drop Inn

'How good to see a full-length, properly developed story in which the canvas is broad and well filled with characters. She gives you not merely the incidents but the thoughts and reactions of all concerned'—*Parents*